CAR SUSPENSION

CAR SUSPENSION

REPAIR, MAINTENANCE AND MODIFICATION

JULIAN SPENDER

THE CROWOOD PRESS

First published in 2019 by
The Crowood Press Ltd
Ramsbury, Marlborough
Wiltshire SN8 2HR

enquiries@crowood.com

www.crowood.com

British Library Cataloguing-in-Publication Data
A catalogue record for this book is available from the British Library.

ISBN 978 1 78500 661 6

Dedication
Dedicated to my wife and children for putting up with my long hours
in the garden shed, every Sunday, for well over a year. Without your
patience and understanding this book could never have been
completed.

Disclaimer
Safety is of the utmost importance in every aspect of an automotive
workshop. The practical procedures and the tools and equipment
used in automotive workshops are potentially dangerous. Tools should
be used in strict accordance with the manufacturer's recommended
procedures and current health and safety regulations. The author
and publisher cannot accept responsibility for any accident or injury
caused by following the advice given in this book.

Designed and typeset by Guy Croton Publishing Services,
West Malling, Kent

Printed and bound in India by Parksons Graphics

CONTENTS

INTRODUCTION   6

1 WHY IS SUSPENSION NECESSARY?   8

2 TYPES OF SUSPENSION AND HOW THEY WORK   16

3 REPAIRING SUSPENSION SYSTEMS   50

4 MODIFYING A SUSPENSION SYSTEM   86

INDEX   175

INTRODUCTION

The aim of this book is that it appeals to novice and professional alike. It doesn't have too many complicated formulas, and it isn't the 'go-to' book for a Formula One team looking for the next advantage in suspension. However, it does provide a concise overview of the different types of suspension. The reader may not be mechanically minded, but is perhaps a keen driver – or they may be actively involved in some form of motor sport, and may find that the text refreshes some basic concepts, or provides a platform for lateral thought.

Above all I have tried to keep the subject interesting, without getting too bogged down in the complicated mathematics that govern the subject. By using examples at the extremes of suspension applications, the reader will understand that the most important thing is to set out a clear objective, and to work to achieve that. Moreover, just as in many spheres, initial objectives may not be met first time, and a process of testing, analysis and modification may be required. Rinse and repeat until the objective is met – or finally realize that

A 'stanced' VW Polo showing stretched tyres, oversized wheels, and lots of negative camber to get the wheel to fit in the arch. If you want a car that looks like this when stationary and you want to clear a speed bump, then air or hydraulic suspension is ideal. However, if the tyres are stretched too far on the wheels, they become dangerous, so if you like this look it is important to keep the speed low around corners. Tyres are usually larger in width than the rim, or are possibly the same size.

A Flawed Design: The Magnificent Auto Union Racecar

The Auto Union Racecar was a V16-engined monster of a car, and much credit must go to the drivers who completed races around the legendary green hell of the Nürburgring in one of these frankly dangerous cars. At the time the rear suspension was considered advanced, but the limited understanding of kinematics at the time meant that the oversteer the car experienced was never fully understood. If a layman from the modern day went back in time with an inexpensive suspension design program on a laptop, he could have told them that the rear sus-pension design was inherently flawed. It had a badly located roll centre, terrible camber control, and jacking forces that multiplied in such a way that the car could snap into an unrecoverable spin. Throw in low grip tyres and the capability for over 320km/h (200mph), and it's not surprising this car took the life of Rosemeyer in 1938 during an attempt on the land speed record on a German autobahn. Later in the book we'll look briefly at chassis dynamics, and discover how steady-state understeer is designed into modern vehicles.

Auto Union Type C – the rear suspension design, roll centre location and weight distribution made this car very dangerous.

there is an inherent design flaw in the vehicle, which cannot easily be solved.

As well as well-known shocks and springs, there are other types of suspension system available, and this book will consider the virtues and foibles of these, too. Furthermore, rather than being a repair manual for various different types of suspension – this market is well served by workshop repair manuals – hopefully it will help the reader think about how the suspension on a particular vehicle could be modified to achieve the effect they want.

It will also help them understand that suspension is often an area of compromise, and making an advantageous change in one area can often result in a down side in another. For example, if you decide you want a road-legal race car, it is perfectly easy to make it super on circuit, but it will be downright dangerous on a winding B road with a wet surface. And if you want a road-legal car that can be lowered 100mm (4in) when stationary, but will still clear speed bumps, clearly this cannot be achieved using simple springs and dampers.

CHAPTER ONE

WHY IS SUSPENSION NECESSARY?

The definition for suspension in the *Oxford English Dictionary* is as follows:

> The system of springs and shock absorbers by which a vehicle is supported on its wheels.

The fundamental reason for suspension is to partially protect the driver of the vehicle from the disrupting effects of the inconsistencies of the road surface beneath the vehicle. The suspended wheel, tyre and hub assembly is able to move over the irregularities in the road surface whilst maintaining grip between the tyre and the road, and causing minimal disruption to the driver within the vehicle. So arguably the first job of suspension is to provide ride comfort. However, as vehicles have advanced in design, the modern suspension system tries to find the ultimate compromise between comfort, handling grip and engagement.

A BRIEF HISTORY OF SUSPENSION

The simplest form of suspension was first used on horse-drawn carriages. Straps made of iron chain or leather would be used to allow the carriage to move independently of the wheels below. If you look at the carriage in the picture you can see the leather strap facilitating, and limiting, transverse movement of the carriage.

The first patent logged for the use of springs was by Obadiah Elliot in 1804 for mounting carriages on elliptical springs attached to the axle – though this, of course, was not the first use of a spring. In ancient times the principle of the spring would have been used for siege weapons, such as a catapult. However, the use of springs to provide suspension eluded these earliest of engineers.

Horse-drawn carriage.

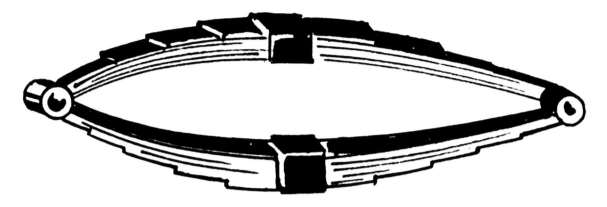

Elliptical leaf spring.

Brush Runabout.

Once the elliptical spring came into being, it rapidly became the most popular suspension solution for carriages, and latterly vehicles. Although leaf springs are rarely found in cars today, they are still popular in larger commercial vehicles.

Next was the coil spring, first seen in a vehicle application in 1906 on the Brush Runabout.

Coil springs are now the most widely used spring component in modern suspension systems – although notably the Chevrolet Corvette has been using a transverse leaf spring in its rear suspension right up to the present day, citing packaging benefits, and the durability of the now composite material leaf.

THE FUNCTION OF DAMPING

Although, as we have seen, the *Oxford English Dictionary* begins its definition of suspension as 'The system of springs and shock absorbers…', the correct term for a shock absorber is actually a damper. This is because its function is to damp the oscillation of the spring. However, with early suspension systems it was quickly realized that although they made uneven surfaces more comfortable, they still had an Achilles heel, which was discovered when velocity was increased. The undamped spring would start to work like a pendulum with each movement in one direction, being compensated for by movement in the other. By travelling faster and faster, movements would eventually go beyond the spring's maximum travel (to go 'coilbound'), and possibly result in the occupants being flung from the carriage, or the carriage turning over.

The first to use a form of damper on an automobile was Mors, in 1902. Although this is a book on suspension, it is probably a safe bet that you like engines as well, and it is useful to refer back to the specification of the Mors engine, to put the era in context. It was powered by a 10-litre, V4 side-valve engine, with magneto ignition and dry sump lubrication. It would reach a heady 950rpm and produce just 6bhp per litre, making in total 60bhp. A Honda S2000 engine makes 240bhp from 2 litres and hits 9,500rpm! The reason for the comparison is the fact that many cars still use a conventional spring and

hydraulic damper. Although there have been significant advances in suspension technology, in its most basic form the conventional spring and damper looks and performs remarkably like the products of yesteryear.

We will see later in the book how a number of other suspension designs came into being, all of which offer significant advantages over the simple spring and damper. We'll also see how, strangely, they never gained the mass-market appeal that the designers would originally have thought possible.

ONE SUSPENSION SYSTEM FOR ALL SURFACES?

'A picture speaks a thousand words' is a truism in the field of suspension, just like many others. The next three images show three different vehicles, each with varying levels of cornering grip; however, it will be necessary to read the captions in order to appreciate which vehicle corners the fastest.

It then becomes apparent that the kart (which can be bought for as little as £1,000 second-hand) generates significantly more grip than a cutting-edge supercar. So that's it then, we don't really need suspension, and the book can stop here! … If only it were that simple.

The G-force to which the vehicle subjects its occupants is not, as some might think, centrifugal force. A vehicle with tyres is generating something known as 'centripetal force' (from the Latin 'centre' and 'to seek'), which is a force that makes a body follow a curved path. The centripetal force is directed at right angles to the motion, and also along the radius towards the centre of the circular path. We feel this force in the vehicle as it attempts to make us slide across the seat.

Although the kart has no suspension, its chassis is designed to work in harmony with the tyre, and is complex – in fact kart set-up, although it might appear simple, can be just as involved as a car. Sometimes it can seem counter-intuitive to that of a car, but equally, learning how it works can often enable the user to solve a problem in the car's handling, which previously had them stumped.

This superkart is capable of generating cornering forces of over 2G, and it has no suspension whatsoever.

McLaren 600LT: this modern McLaren sports car is generating cornering forces of around 1.7G – it has a sophisticated, hydraulic, computer-controlled suspension.

A standard production car on road tyres cornering at 0.95G. XTREME SPORTS PHOTOGRAPHY

Discovering that a kart with no suspension can corner faster than the modern supercar isn't perhaps entirely fair, because due consideration to modern formula cars has not been given. A modern Formula One car does have a complicated suspension system, and can corner at even higher G-forces than a kart. However, most of this advantage comes from the use of aerodynamics. Thus a modern Formula One car manages the airflow that passes over it, to increase downforce, and the interplay between the lateral grip of the tyre, versus the vertical load on it, is key to making the aerodynamics work correctly. Too much aerodynamic load on the tyre may cause it to fail prematurely, or will decrease outright grip, as the maximum loading of the tyre would have been reached. Too little aerodynamic load will mean that the tyre doesn't reach its optimum grip-versus-load point.

TRAVELLING FAST ON BUMPY SURFACES

So for high speed, smooth circuit use, very little travel seems to work well. However you wouldn't get very far up the side of the mountain in a racing car or a kart.

Unimog 404 chassis showing the extreme wheel articulation available.

The Ariel Nomad, possibly the only vehicle that excels both on and off road.

Maximum speed around a corner is a function of track width and the height of the vehicle's centre of gravity. Thus it is easy to see that an SUV will have a lower theoretical cornering speed than the equivalent car, because the vehicle is higher up and has a higher centre of gravity (although it is usually wider to help prevent it rolling over). Conversely is also easy to visualize how this kind of vehicle should be better off road, with its long wheel travel and off-

road tyres – though that is not, of course, to say that such an appearance is a guarantee of performance. Some cars, however much they look the part, are good neither on road nor off.

The main reason that the vehicle geared for off-road use is superior in such an environment, is the travel and independent nature of the suspension. On off-road surfaces there may be large undulations over a short distance, requiring the suspension to have significant amounts of droop (movement in the downward direction) to meet with the downward direction of the surface, while equally on the opposite wheel there needs to be a large amount of compression travel (movement in the upward direction).

As you can see from the picture opposite, the requirements of suspension for this surface are completely different to that needed for the smooth tarmac of a racetrack. Off-road vehicles not only employ suspension with much more travel, but four-wheel-drive versions make use of differential locking: this locks the drive between the two wheels – much like a race kart, which has no differential and a solid rear axle. With differential locks engaged, the vehicle will not want to turn, but it will have considerably more drive on a slippery and uneven surface.

The latest four-wheel drives use a range of electronic technology to enable them to traverse as wide a range of surfaces as possible, without the driver interaction that would normally be required – although a recent episode of Amazon's *Grand Tour* showed that this kind of technology is not infallible. In fact it demonstrated that the popularity of SUVs on the road has made them severely compromised off-road.

This is the single biggest challenge of suspension. It is extremely hard to take one system and one style of vehicle and make it work in all environments: there has to be an element of compromise. Any vehicle with significant off-road ability will tend to be quite hampered on road. In the next chapter we will also see that, just as the suspension system needs to be fit for purpose, crucially so do the tyres. There are plenty of modern SUVs that look as if they could go off road, but as they are supplied with low-profile summer tyres, they have no real benefit over a car fitted with all-season tyres.

There is arguably one vehicle that crosses the boundary between high performance on road, and high performance off road, and that is the Ariel Nomad. An exquisitely brazed chassis (Gordon Murray's Rocket was also brazed – it gives a stronger joint than welding, and prevents warping) is fitted out with top name components, from the Honda VTEC engine to Bilstein suspension and Alcon brakes. This machine has phenomenal pace both on and off road, and because it is light, the long travel suspension can work in both spheres of operation. Granted, compared to the Atom there is more body roll on road, but the flexibility of the vehicle is a good demonstration of the virtuous circle that comes from light weight.

CHAPTER TWO

TYPES OF SUSPENSION AND HOW THEY WORK

In this chapter we will be looking at the different types of suspension, how they work, and what their benefits are. However, first we must look at tyres.

THE IMPORTANCE OF TYRES

Tyres are often said to be the most important part of the vehicle, and this really is true, assuming that everything else is fit for purpose, and designed from the tyre upwards. For example, there would be no point in building an incredible racing car, optimised for a racing slick tyre, and then entering the first race on road tyres. Likewise, a four-wheel-drive vehicle can never properly operate off road without a specialist tyre – at the very least it would need an all-season tyre, although this would compromise its performance in summer.

When we look at tyres and how they interact with suspension, the subject is nearly as broad as that of suspension itself. Where they are similar is in the quest for a solution that is fit for purpose.

THE COMPLEXITIES OF GRIP

For a racing tyre we are looking for maximum lateral grip, and a favourable set of characteristics to enable the driver to maximize performance over the life of the tyres. Lateral G-Force readings may be as much as 5G with aerodynamic downforce. For an off-road tyre the ability to grip on slippery surfaces while still offering good performance on tarmac is crucial. The off-road tyre is not focused on high lateral G, and will be lucky to achieve 0.6G. The tyre generates lateral grip by interacting with the surface it is on.

There are two fundamental types of grip: adhesion and hysteresis. Adhesion results from the interaction between the tyre and the surface of the road. When the road is wet, adhesive grip is reduced. This would also occur with oil on the road surface, or any substance that reduces the coefficient of friction.

The other type of grip is hysteresis driven. As the tyre doesn't give back all the load put into it, it suffers from hysteresis, which means there is a delay in its reaction to the surface. Although at first this situation doesn't sound as if it would generate grip, what the tyre is actually doing is creeping over the surface and interlocking with it over its vertical imperfections, and the delay in the tyre's reaction to the surface actually increases its grip and also temperature. The level of hysteresis – it is generally increased with the softer compounds – dictates the performance and behaviour of the tyre.

The shape of a tyre and its tread are specifically designed to work on a chosen surface. Thus a slick racing tyre for smooth tarmac will have no tread at all. A wet racing tyre will be similar, but is made from a softer compound, with large grooves to drain out water. A winter tyre is often characterized by being siped. Siping is the process of cutting thin slits across a rubber surface, or in this case small grooves across larger tread elements to improve traction in wet or icy conditions. More sipes give more traction in snow or mud, and also on cold, wet surfaces. Typically, wide, straight grooves have a low noise level and good water removal. Siping was invented and patented in 1923 under the name of John F. Sipe, but it was his son Harry Sipe who applied the technology to pneumatic tyres.

Interestingly there is a lizard called a gecko, whose ability to grip on a vertical surface works in a similar way. A gecko foot under magnification can be seen to have microscopic hairs that effectively increase the grip between its feet and the surface, and enable it literally to walk up walls and even a vertical glass pane. However, as is often the case, there are compro-

Gecko foot showing the microscopic hairs that improve its grip.

mises, and although a gecko is an excellent all-surface specialist, it isn't the fastest lizard.

Similarly, winter tyres, and 'mud and snow' tyres, may have thousands of sipes and give good traction in difficult conditions, but on a hot summer's day when both the tyre and the road surface are warm they may feel 'squirmy'.

Incidentally in snowy conditions it is interesting to note how much grip you get from a space-saver wheel and tyre, as supplied for a spare tyre on most modern cars. If you have one fitted and you are driving in snow, you will soon appreciate that the space-saver is the only tyre keying in to the surface.

THE CIRCLE OF GRIP

The 'circle of grip' is a circular representation of the capability of a tyre (see diagram). Most of the time when driving, a tyre is combining more than one force. For example, as

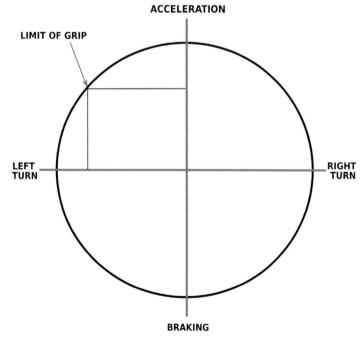

Diagram showing the 'circle of grip'.

you enter a corner you are decelerating, and generally would use a technique called 'trail braking', where you will be turning the car into the corner whilst gently releasing the brake. At this point the tyre is having to cope with both deceleration and cornering forces. If a tyre is capable of generating 700kg of lateral force for 450kg of vertical loading, the maximum G-force generated will be 700/450=1.55G. At maximum speed around a left or right turn with no deceleration or acceleration the adhesive limit will be on the edge of the circle at the left or right turn location.

However, by adding acceleration or deceleration forces, the maximum lateral grip is then compromised. If you are already at maximum lateral acceleration you cannot add any acceleration or deceleration without straying beyond the circle: any more loading will result in a slide. Only a combination of acceleration or deceleration, and lateral grip that falls within the circle, is achievable. In the diagram the blue line shows a combination of lateral force and acceleration that is right on the edge of the circle. In this instance no more lateral force is available without a reduction in acceleration.

If ever you have driven 'on the limit' on a circuit you will know the feeling of breaching the circle of grip, which will be manifested as either understeer, oversteer, or even a four-wheel drift, depending on the set-up of the car.

Typical G-Force Figures from Tyres

The tyre is the governing factor here, however chassis stiffness and set-up are crucial to ensuring that both the front and rear tyres work to the best of their ability. In addition, aerodynamics that generate downforce provide what is known as 'free grip'. Generally speaking, most typical road tyres in a modern car will generate approximately 0.85G. Softer and 'grippier' tyres will be able to push this to 1G, which is about the limit on a typical road tyre. Then there are 'track day'-style tyres, which try to combine the benefits of a slick racing tyre with a road-legal tread. These tyres are typically three to five times softer than a normal road tyre, and with a well-designed chassis will generate something like 1.2G to 1.4G. A kart with no

suspension and slick tyres can generate over 2G, and F1 can reach 5G. Nevertheless, however much grip the tyre can generate, the overall lateral and longitudinal mix is still governed by the circle of grip.

Drifting Wastes Grip

With the circle, it is easy to understand how a car that is drifting cannot generate as much lateral grip as one that isn't (assuming all other things are equal). When a car is drifting sideways, accelerative forces have overcome the lateral grip capability of the tyre, to the point where the tyre is often spinning as well as gripping. The reason for this is the contact patch given by extremely wide tyres. A typical drift car will run much wider wheels and tyres than standard, as these offer maximum lateral grip at the expense of tractive grip, which is exactly what the drifter needs.

The Right Contact Patch

If you have a flat tyre and replace it temporarily with the space-saver from the boot, you might think that its grip would be easily overcome both acceleratively and laterally. In fact when fitted, the space-saver has the same size contact patch as the wheel you removed, it is just that the shape of the patch changes – the space-saver contact patch is narrow (laterally) but fatter. The (flat) tyre you remove gives a contact patch that is wide laterally but thin. So although in a picture the contact patches might look very different, the area is the same.

Pneumatic Trail

The trail-like effect to the contact patch when subject to vertical load is known as pneumatic trail. It is generated as the tyre finds its grip over the surface. Specifically, it is the distance generated by the forces of side-slip that occurs behind the geometric centre of the contact patch.

Theoretically, then, wider tyres will have no benefit. But we all know that this is not true, as a wider tyre can resist cornering forces better. However, it is not as good at straight-line traction and deceleration. This is easy to visualize in your mind as you will no doubt be aware how a wide wheel and tyre offers less grip on slippery surfaces.

Diagram to illustrate the different contact patch shape between a narrow and a wide tyre.

CONTACT PATCH OF NARROW TYRE

CONTACT PATCH OF WIDE TYRE

BELOW: *A dragster tyre is tall and narrow as compared to a racing-car tyre, which is shorter and wider to give maximum accelerative grip.*
RICHARD SHUTE

BOTH HAVE THE SAME CONTACT PATCH AREA

Tyre Grip Versus Vertical Load

Some tyre manufacturers are able to provide load data versus lateral force. This is very useful when designing or modifying suspension and chassis. Essentially, if you know what the tyre is capable of, then the suspension can be built and designed around it. So if you aren't already sure which tyre you are going to run, then see if any of the suppliers on the shortlist of tyres you have selected can provide vertical versus lateral load data for their product.

The graph shows the varying lateral force generated by a tyre at different vertical loadings. For example, as you can see, the 450kg vertical loading can generate a much greater lateral force for a given slip angle than the 300kg vertical loading – *but* the lateral force diminishes more quickly as the limits of the tyre are approached. This load data would be for a racing tyre: as you can see, at a 450kg vertical load the tyre generates 700kg lateral load. Divide 700/450 to get 1.55, and this tyre could generate 1.55G of grip.

Armed with this data it is much easier to work out what kind of spring and anti-roll bar rates will be required to maximize cornering force.

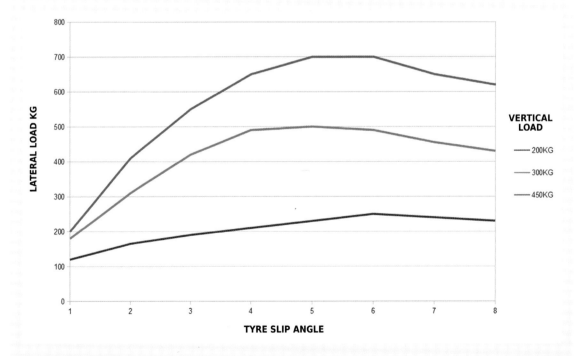

Tyre load data, showing the lateral grip a tyre can generate versus its vertical load.

Another good example would be a dragster tyre, which is comparatively narrow, as cornering is irrelevant and maximum tractive grip is the aim. The tyres are generally very soft and also inflated to a low pressure – it is possible to see the huge forces at work as a dragster launches off the line.

In the picture on the previous page you can see the effect of a high G launch on a specialist drag-racing tyre, which is sometimes known as a 'wrinkle wall', the idea being that rather than wheel spin, the tyre torques up like a clockwork motor, and then releases its energy, resulting in a faster getaway from the line. In addition the tyre expands radially, which affects the gearing on the vehicle.

Managing the Circle of Grip

Recently a leading magazine ran a feature on a certain Rob Wilson, a New Zealander who has had a long and varied career in motor sport. What was interesting is that allegedly half of the F1 grid have called on his services – which might seem surprising, as you would expect them to know what they were doing already. However, it demonstrates how crucial it is to a fast lap time to manage the overall grip available: the old adage 'smooth is fast' is more appropriate than ever. As a driver you have to manage the weight transfer around the car and around the tyres constantly, and in different ways, to ensure fast progress. This explains why the traditional racing line is not always the fastest.

TYRE TESTING – THE MAGIC FORMULA

The most popular formula that is used to test tyres is the so-called 'magic formula'. These formulae were models originally developed by Hans B. Pacejka, and so named because there was no solid scientific basis for the structure of the equations. However, as an empirical model the magic formula works very well. Each tyre is characterized by a number of coefficients, and these are then used within the formula to calculate the force generated by the tyre in response to vertical load. The parameters used in this formula are designed to offer a good representation of what is actually happening when the tyre interacts with the

ground. Whilst the model is significantly simpler than the physics actually involved, it is one that is nonetheless intimidating for most.

The general form for the formula is:
R(k)=d-sin{c-arctan[b (1-e)k+e-arctan(bk)]}

The Overturning Moment

Tyre models are particularly useful at modelling the possibility of rollover. With the seemingly unending appetite for SUV-style vehicles, the greater risks of rollover must be managed. Most normal cars (and particularly high performance cars) will slide before they roll (in most circumstances). SUV-style vehicles, with their higher centre of gravity, are much more prone to roll over. This phenomenon can actually be measured on a tyre-testing machine, where the model used will be honed to ensure the vehicle can be developed to ensure it won't roll over during real world testing.

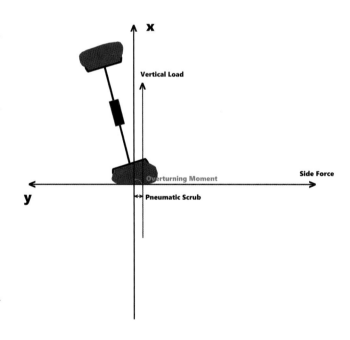

Diagram showing the overturning moment present under heavy cornering loads.

The factors at play are the height of the centre of gravity, the roll stiffness, the track width, and the overturning moment of the tyres. As a tyre slips across the surface it also moves sideways. At low levels of lateral force the tyre isn't distorting greatly and only a fraction of its contact patch is in use, so the overturning moment will be negative. This is a result of the pneumatic scrub being negative in relation to the lateral force. At higher lateral forces, the full contact patch is used and the pneumatic scrub is positive, and the overturning moment is formed between the longitudinal axis of the wheel contact point and the centreline of the tyre contact patch.

In order to reduce the likelihood of SUV rollover, wide tyres are fitted. A narrower tyre will reach a full tread contact earlier. That is why the switch point between the negative overturning moment and the positive overturning moment will occur earlier. So logically, of course, this means that a wider tyre will reduce the chance of rollover. Now it is easy to understand that the massive wheels and tyres on a car of this class aren't all there for show, but actually have an important part to play in keeping the vehicle upright.

SPRINGS

In the introduction we saw how elliptical springs, and then later coil springs, became the most common form of suspension. The spring is a seemingly simple component, which does a remarkable job without fuss: in fact its performance is usually taken for granted until such time that it breaks – at which point the owner may feel that it hasn't lasted long enough. It is certainly not uncommon for a spring to last more than ten years. Over 100,000 miles (160,000km) at an average speed of 40mph (65km/h) and a suspension frequency of 2Hz amounts to eighteen million cycles of compression and extension. In reality this fairly simplistic calculation doesn't take into account the true punishment the spring receives: large compressions and heavy loads mean that this simple item is working hard and continuously every moment you drive.

WHAT SPRINGS ARE MADE OF

Springs are made from a wide range of materials, from simple carbon steel to more complicated steel alloys – even exotic materials such as beryllium and titanium are used. However, by far the most common material is chrome silicon, or chrome vanadium for suspension springs. Both of these names refer to the materials the steel is alloyed with. Perhaps surprisingly the amounts added are very small. Thus a typical chrome silicon steel will have a carbon content (C) of 0.5 per cent, silicon (Si) of 1.2 per cent, and chrome (Cr) of 0.6 per cent. A typical chrome vanadium steel will have C of 0.5 per cent, Cr of 0.8 per cent, and vanadium (V) of 0.15 per cent. But although these percentages are very small, they make a dramatic difference to the performance of the metal.

Springs made from simple carbon steel just wouldn't be up to the task, although they do still appear on the market, particularly where counterfeiting is concerned. There are many strong brand names in the market for springs, and because counterfeiting is a real problem for many of them, always ensure you buy springs from an official source to avoid the possibility of counterfeit goods.

WINDING A SPRING

The spring material is wound into shape hot or cold. Generally speaking, for automotive applications springs are cold wound. Only very thick wire diameters tend to be hot formed. The critical dimensions are wire diameter, where naturally the thicker the wire diameter, the stiffer the spring will be. The next factor will be the number of coils: this perhaps seems counter-intuitive, but a reduced number of coils will result in a stiffer spring. In addition to the number of coils and the wire diameter, the next factor in determining the rate of the spring is the inner diameter: the larger the diameter of the spring, the softer it will be.

SHOT PEENING

After the spring has been wound into shape, stresses will have been created in the material, and if it were used in this state the spring would quickly break. Therefore in order to relieve stresses in the material, it is tempered by heat treatment. In addition, high quality spring manufacturers will then shot peen the product to relieve stress. Shot peening is a process where the metal is bombarded by a myriad of tiny metallic or ceramic balls. It is similar to sandblasting, but it works using the principle of plastic deformation rather than abrasion. The barrage of tiny balls changes the surface structure of the metal and creates what is known as a 'compressive residual stress layer'. The objective is to increase the lifetime of the spring. Stress fractures normally originate from imperfections in the original surface, and shot peening prevents this.

The effectiveness of shot peening was assessed in a study completed by the SAE Fatigue Design and Evaluation Committee. They showed what shot peening can do for welds (you will probably already know that every weld introduces a weakness). The study claimed that regular welds would fail after 250,000 cycles, whereas welds that had been shot peened would fail after 2.5 million cycles, and that failure would occur outside the weld area.

PROTECTIVE TREATMENT

Once made, the spring is then treated for corrosion protection: usually the wire will be galvanized, then powder coated with colour, and then a clear coat of lacquer applied on top.

Other types of spring are still used on cars, such as the leaf spring or torsion bar. Although these styles of spring are visually different, great similarity exists in their metallurgy and in the manufacturing process.

RUBBER SUSPENSION

If you take the word of polyurethane bush manufacturers, you could easily be forgiven for thinking that rubber was a completely outmoded material, and only used because it is cheap. However, it is noteworthy that Issigonis had a particular problem to solve with the Mini, and rubber came into the solution. Whilst being a small light car, the Mini was still remarkably roomy inside, which meant that its load-carrying capacity represented a much greater proportion of the vehicle weight than other models of the time. As

the vehicle weight is increased, the effective suspension stiffness is decreased. In addition, as the load is increased, suspension deflection will increase. If the Mini were to carry four passengers and a modest amount of luggage in the boot successfully, it would need fairly stiff suspension springs. This then meant that, even when lightly loaded, the suspension would be too stiff. In addition the ride height change would be unacceptable.

To get round this problem, Alex Moulton invented a rubber cone-type suspension for the Mini, the remarkable characteristics of rubber making such an elegant solution possible, while at the same time creating the handling legend that is the original Mini. One of the unique properties of rubber compared to steel is its high level of hysteresis, which means that, to a degree, rubber is self-damping.

Hysteresis in a spring is where a material gives back less energy than was put into it. A steel spring has very low hysteresis, so for a large compressive input there is an almost equally large extension output. Undamped, the energy will take a long time to dissipate, a bit like Newton's cradle. Some suspension designs will allow you to drive them with the dampers disconnected, and this is quite an experience – but don't drive on the road with steel springs and no dampers!

By using rubber cones on the Mini suspension, the car was able to have a smooth ride with one person, and yet could still carry four adults in comfort, without compromising ground clearance, or resulting in bottoming out. Two principles were at work here to make this possible. The first was the rising rate of rubber: under a greater compressive load, the effective spring rate of the rubber would increase. This is what supported the car with a full load. Secondly, because of rubber's greater hysteresis, the extra spring rate of the suspension is partly self-damped. Picture, for a moment, a conventional spring that doubled in rate. This would need the damper to offer significantly more rebound force to control the spring, and specifying a damper for such a system would be fraught with compromise.

The difference in response from the vehicle with just the driver, compared to fully loaded, is particularly noticeable in roll control. Even with the use of anti-roll bars, a heavily loaded vehicle, which consequently has softer suspension, will tend to roll much more.

Rubber solves most of the problems through its material response, and presented the perfect solution to the Mini's suspension conundrum. As well as allowing the extra load to be carried, when it came to cornering, the rising rate of the rubber cone suspension delivered increased roll resistance. It also worked the tyre harder, leading to more outright grip. As a result, the Mini was truly a phenomenon – it was able to upstage much more powerful cars, and its legendary grip and handling even saw it win the toughest challenge of them all, the Mille Miglia.

It sounds as if rubber is the solution to all our problems on the suspension front. However, there is always a downside. On a larger vehicle it will be harder to engineer the balance between comfort and handling, and hysteresis, which generates heat, will also be an issue in larger, heavier vehicles. We do,

however, still see rubber used in nearly all road-going production vehicles as a bushing material. This is why aftermarket bushes are popular, as they can provide a reduction in compliance, which may increase overall vehicle speed round a corner.

INVESTIGATING HYSTERESIS

The word 'hysteresis' is derived from ancient Greek, and literally means 'shortcoming' or 'deficiency'. It describes the lag between an input and a consequent output. However, as well as lagging behind, the effect may well be less than the cause.

This is most easily seen when looking at an elastic substance. If you take a rubber band and then add weight to it gradually, measuring the amount of stretch in the band as the weight is added, it would be relatively straightforward to draw a conclusion that a certain amount of weight would lead to a certain amount of deflection. Unfortunately, as the weights are removed, if measurements are taken again, it is

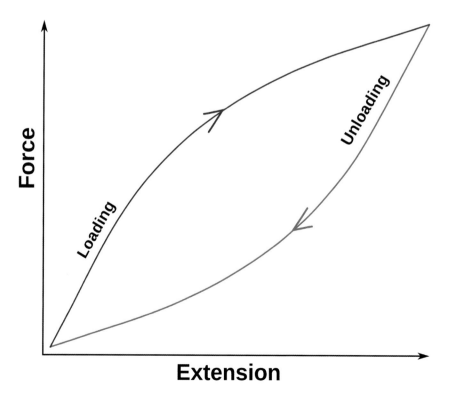

A hysteresis loop showing the loss of energy in the middle of the loop.

possible to see that the elastic band does not return to the same position it was in before the weight was added. Therefore not all of the initial energy input is being returned.

In essence, more energy is required to stretch the band in the first instance, and the excess energy required is turned into heat. If this behaviour is plotted into a graph, it creates what is known as the 'hysteresis loop'. The area between the curves shows the lost energy, which turns to heat and is not given back when the force is unloaded.

Different materials have different reactions to load. Generally speaking, greater stiffness in the material will lead to a larger area between loading and unloading. Therefore, switching to a stiffer bushing material can create more heat in the material. At lower temperatures rubber and polyurethane will have a larger hysteresis area, but more ability to absorb energy. As temperatures rise, the hysteresis area will reduce (that is, it will give more back of the input force). However, at the same time the energy handling levels are reduced overall.

Rubber deals with heat much better than polyurethane. In fact rubber's ability to flex, together with its hysteresis, means it is employed to provide a smooth connection between the suspension and bodyshell. Furthermore, used in the articulating joints, shock bushes and top mounts, rubber gives the chassis engineer an easy solution to noise problems.

However, hysteresis and a flexible joint are not always required. Polyurethane material bushings are predominantly sold on the aftermarket as a solution to some of the weaknesses of rubber bushings. As a material it has much less hysteresis than rubber, which is fortunate, as it doesn't react well to high temperatures. The mix of the material can be changed. The polyol is the soft flexible element. If you imagine a bungie cord, the metal hooks could be likened to the isocyanates: these create links and connections with the polyol, in turn creating polymers. Different mixes can give soft and pliant or tough and hard textures.

Hysteresis is something that needs to be considered in many areas of the suspension system. Sometimes it can be used to your advantage, at other times it is your enemy. For example, a car that

regularly comes into contact with a bump stop may overheat its tyre, but equally a bump stop can be an effective way of working a tyre harder. How does the bump stop react to load? What is its force deflection curve? The tyre itself relies to a certain extent on hysteresis for grip. A very hard tyre with low hysteresis won't generate as much heat as a softer, stickier tyre designed to work at greater slip angles (think of slip angle in terms of the hysteresis curve).

DAMPERS (SHOCK ABSORBERS)

Early dampers used friction, and sometimes mass to control the spring; nowadays the majority of dampers are fundamentally oil based with differing gas charges. Simple, cheaper, oil only dampers are still used, and many twin-tube dampers use a simple gas bag rather than a gas charge.

Dampers work with springs (whether air or metal). They are often called shock absorbers, but technically they aren't absorbing shock, they are damping the oscillations of the spring. However, dampers can be used with electronic controls to mimic the effect of a spring, and in a fully active suspension they can even replace the spring altogether, although this is seldom seen in practice.

DAMPING FORCES

A damper works in two directions, known as compression and extension, and/or bump and rebound. The compression force is felt by the wheel hitting a bump, by braking (on the front axle) or by acceleration (on the rear axle). It is also felt on the outside wheel during cornering.

The rebound force is there to control the energy in the spring as it decompresses. A way of noting if rebound control is unacceptable is if the tyre thumps hard into the ground when moving off a kerb, and also if the car body bobs up and down like a boat.

Rebound forces tend to be two to three times higher in the damper's dyno plot than compression force. The compression force is there to aid the spring in absorbing the initial bump force. This is probably why the term 'shock absorber' is used so much. However, once that spring has moved, it

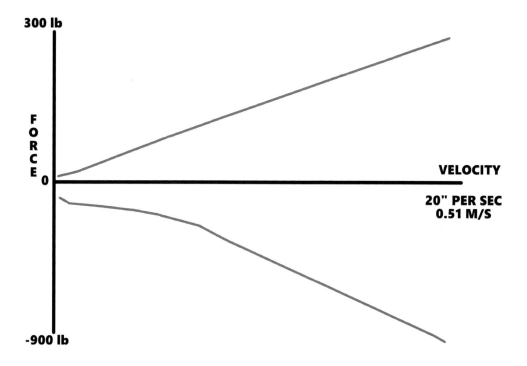

An example of a force versus velocity curve for a damper, compression top (less force), rebound bottom (more force).

now has stored energy. If the damper wasn't there to control this, the wheel would push the body back up and the car would start to bounce. It is the element of body control as well as spring control that makes rebound forces higher than compression.

Racing applications may tend to have a lower ratio, closer to 2:1, whereas for a smooth road ride a ratio of 3:1 is more common. This is because on a smooth track plenty of low speed compression adds stability to the vehicle and makes it feel sharp when turning, particularly from left to right. If you were to have the same set-up on a road car it would be very unforgiving over the bumps.

When we talk about speed with dampers we mean the velocity. Dampers are rated according to their force at a given velocity, or also force versus deflection. The two tests produce totally different shaped plots, and damper dyno plots are a little harder to grasp than the power and torque outputs of an engine.

As you can see from the velocity versus force dyno chart, the damper responds to increasing velocity with increasing force. If this motion is linear, the damper will be said to have a linear piston. It looks fairly simple, but as we'll see in Chapter 4, the real skill is in shaping this curve to suit both the tyre, the surface *and the driver.*

Without a damper, a spring would quite happily oscillate wildly, as the energy slowly dissipates through friction in mounting points and the material itself. If there were no friction, then your car would do a good impersonation of Newton's cradle. If you have an opportunity to drive a car with no effective damping, do so slowly, and preferably not on a public road – you'll be amazed at the amount of energy generated by a speed hump, for example. The damper can be valved to effectively control the spring's energy, and done correctly the body control will be exemplary, and the car will appear to dismiss bumps as if they aren't there. It should be noted that good bump-stop design is often crucial here.

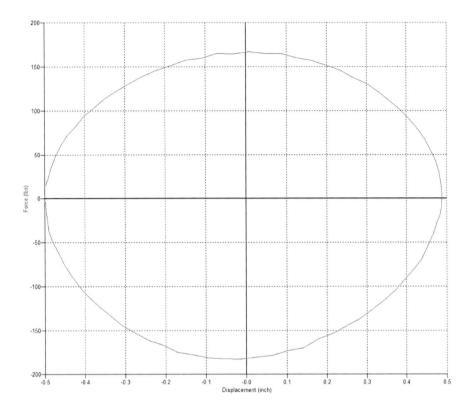

A force deflection curve for a competition damper (note the nearly 1:1 ratio
for compression and rebound force).

Scientifically, damping is denoted by ζ (zeta). A system can be undamped (ζ=0), underdamped (ζ<1), critically damped (ζ=1) or overdamped (ζ>1).

Logically, you might think that critical damping would be the objective. However, experience shows that this creates too much stiffness in the suspension, effectively preventing it from working correctly.

As well as damping the sprung and unsprung mass of the vehicle, we also have the tyre, which is undamped. In fact due to the hysteresis curve of rubber, the tyre is, to a degree, self-damped – though let's not forget it is full of air (or nitrogen, if you're serious). The springs and anti-roll bars provide their force based on deflection; the damper, on the other hand, provides its force based on velocity. This means it is only providing force when things are moving. It is now possible to start to see the interplay between the tyre, spring and damper. The energy in the tyre is also experienced by the damper. As you will dis-

cover by the end of the book it is the combination of damper, spring and tyre that provides the advantage to get ahead in competition.

So in effect you have two springs (the spring and the tyre) and two dampers – the hydraulic one and the rubber in the tyre. Then you have all four corners of the car. This is then further complicated by the fact that as well as dealing with the resonant frequencies of the spring and tyre, the damper must also cope with longitudinal movement from acceleration and braking, lateral movement from roll due to cornering forces, as well heave from the body mass, and yaw. There are effectively six degrees of motion going on. The first three are rotational motions – these occur about a fixed axis and are known as roll, pitch and yaw. Translational movement considers the motion by which a body shifts from one point in space to another, and the three degrees of motion are known as heave, surge and sway.

Something that might strike you here is that technically roll and sway are not the same thing.

They are, however, used interchangeably by anti-roll bar and sway-bar manufacturers. Generally speaking in Europe it is anti-roll, and in America and Australia it is anti-sway.

Regardless of the semantics over the terminology, adding a large amount of anti-roll stiffness definitely gives the damper more work to do over single wheel bumps. When you consider all the forces the damper has to contend with, you can then appreciate how they make a massive difference to the way a car handles.

HYDRAULIC DAMPERS

There are two fundamental types of hydraulic damper in use on today's cars: mono-tube and twin-tube, and their names are exactly descriptive of the key difference between them. The simplistic drawing below perhaps shows the differences between the two types more clearly than a cutaway drawing.

THE TWIN-TUBE DAMPER

The twin-tube design looks more complicated, so we'll deal with that first. The damper uses the incompressible nature of the oil to provide resistance, as the oil is forced through a small orifice. As the piston moves up and down, oil is displaced. This occurs in the high-pressure tube: if the unit were completely sealed with no room for expansion, it couldn't operate. The outer tube therefore allows for expansion of the oil, and the expansion area is sometimes filled with low-pressure gas, or a gas bag, or simply air from the atmosphere. The passage of flow between the inner and outer tubes is controlled by the base or foot valve. In extreme operational conditions, the heat generated by the piston is harder to manage in this design, because the piston is smaller and the outside air is not in direct contact with the oil behind the outer casing.

The twin-tube design makes up the majority of dampers on road cars. Although it looks more complicated than the mono-tube design, it is in fact

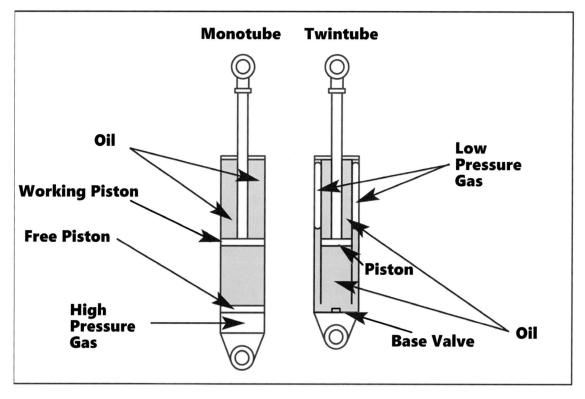

Mono-tube and twin-tube damper cutaway.

cheaper to manufacture. It is also a more forgiving design because it is not relying on a high-pressure gas seal to function correctly. In the United Kingdom, no test is done in the annual MOT for correct damper operation. They are checked for oil leakage, and this is a failure point; however, some oil loss from a twin-tube damper is normal, particularly in its first few hours of operation after transit.

As no test is done on the damper itself, a large number of cars in the UK are driving round with worn dampers, which dramatically reduces the safety of the vehicle. Nevertheless it is a feature of the twin-tube damper that even with significant wear and oil loss, it can usually provide enough rebound damping to stop the vehicle from bouncing up and down continuously. Because of this it is common for drivers to think that the lifetime of a damper is longer than it actually is.

The design of the twin-tube damper means it must only operate in a vertical position. Double-wishbone suspension installations may see 20- to 45-degree angles, which is acceptable. However, they cannot be operated upside down. If you have an old damper, try inverting it, then testing the operation: you will find the piston starts to 'slip' as the air or gas within the damper starts to mix and the base valve can no longer operate.

The benefits of the twin-tube damper are as follows:

• The outer tube can sustain damage without necessarily affecting the operation of the damper
• The cost of production is lower, and the requirement for high gas pressurization is eliminated
• The unit can produce a longer stroke for a given installation height, due to having only one piston
• The lack of the high gas pressure chamber means there is no increase in working spring rate, so the twin-tube will often tend to offer a smoother ride. That said, when comparing it back-to-back with the mono-tube equipped vehicle, the latter will often tend to feel much more sophisticated in its damping responses, due to the high gas pressure
• The lack of high gas pressure reduces the load on seals, and friction

• It is relatively easy to engineer a single combined adjustment for compression and rebound via the base valve
• A large range of force adjustment is permissible via the base valve adjuster

The downsides of the twin-tube damper are as follows:

• Cavitation is the main downside to the twin-tube damper, where inevitably the piston is actually working in an emulsion of oil and gas. A fairly significant reduction in overall performance is found as a result, which gets worse as the oil heats
• At small, high speed inputs the piston can experience some slip and inconsistencies in response
• Due to the piston residing in the smaller pressure tube it is necessarily much smaller than its mono-tube cousin. In reality the piston is approximately half the size
• Due to the smaller oil capacity, together with the lack of direct cooling to the piston, heat management is reduced

THE MONO-TUBE DAMPER

The mono-tube design looks altogether simpler, and it is. Nevertheless it does require specialist machining and build techniques, together with material quality of the highest grade, to make a reliable damper. This makes it more expensive to produce, and arguably, although not conclusively, less relevant to low-cost mass production. Mono-tube dampers tend to be found on high performance cars. Within the single tube design we have a working piston, much like that in the twin-tube, albeit considerably larger in diameter – often twice the size. Moving on either side of the piston through the shim stack and orifices, is the oil. This is then separated by a floating or free piston, which is in turn holding back a volume of high pressure gas. The gas, being compressible, adds a springing effect, and naturally increases in rate with more compression. That is to say, it gets stiffer with deflection. This is a unique property of the mono-tube damper.

In turn, the high pressure gas also ensures that cavitation is greatly reduced – that is, the foaming of the oil, particularly when heavily loaded and when the oil is already hot. Luckily, because the mono-tube has a larger piston, and the oil is in direct contact with the outer casing, it is also superior in this area.

Due to its design, the mono-tube relies on the integrity of the high gas pressure chamber. If this chamber is breached due to a failure of the free piston or seal, then the gas will move to the other side of the working piston, or will even leave the casing if this is not sealed. The damper will then cease to function correctly. Generally speaking, when a mono-tube damper fails, the driver is acutely aware of this because the spring will be oscillating wildly.

The mono-tube damper is found much less often as standard equipment as compared to the twin-tube, but significant numbers of aftermarket performance alternatives use the mono-tube principle. One vehicle manufacturer, Mercedes-Benz, uses Bilstein mono-tube dampers on the majority of their cars (Mercedes-Benz also make use of Bilstein's semi-active suspension, as well as using the Citroën hydro-pneumatic system under licence).

The mono-tube damper has a number of key benefits – these are as follows:

- Improved cooling from the single casing – the working piston which is generating heat is in direct contact with the outer casing, enabling efficient cooling
- Unlike the twin-tube unit, the mono-tube can be used in any orientation (so if the dampers are lying flat on a pushrod racing suspension this immediately tells you they must be of mono-tube design)
- The separate gas layer ensures that cavitation of the oil (mixing with gas or air in a twin-tube) is nearly eliminated
- The oil capacity is greater, and this also improves thermal stability together with the single tube's convection connection to the outside air
- The larger piston area, together with the high gas pressure, delivers a more consistent damping response over challenging road conditions

The downsides of the mono-tube damper are as follows:

- The gas in the mono-tube is at very high pressure – this varies depending on the application, but typically is 300psi (20.7 bar) – and causes stress to the seals and increased friction
- The gas also provides a variable additional springing effect – this may or may not be desirable, depending on the application
- Due to the requirement of a working and a free piston, the overall length of the mono-tube unit will be longer, for the same amount of stroke
- If the units incurs damage to the outer casing, this is highly likely to result in a failure of the damper

ADJUSTABLE DAMPERS

SINGLE ADJUSTABLE DAMPER

The idea of an adjustable damper is to provide a range of settings that enable the vehicle to be dialled into the road or track surface.

Both mono-tube and twin-tube dampers are available in a 'single adjuster' format for most applications. As the twin-tube tends to have the adjuster on the base valve, it will be at the bottom of the damper on the side as it sits upright. This will adjust both compression and rebound. A mono-tube damper will have the adjuster running through the inside of the piston rod to a rotary control, usually inline with the damper. This will also adjust compression and rebound. It is best to think of both mechanisms as a bleed to the main piston circuit. In a mono-tube when fully shut (maximum hardness) all oil must pass through the piston and shim stack. As the adjuster is open, then oil bleeds through the piston-rod passage as well as the main piston. In the twin-tube the base valve is always open to some extent as it is a key part of the design, and the damper couldn't operate if the base valve permitted no flow. It is easy to visualize how this subtly different adjuster will tend to have a wider range of adjustment.

The Bilstein damper cutaway shows the bleed valve in the main piston. As the adjuster is set to softer settings, the brass valve turns to open to allow oil to flow through the valve. When the adjuster is shut, all the oil flows through the main piston.

Bilstein mono-tube damper cutaway drawing.

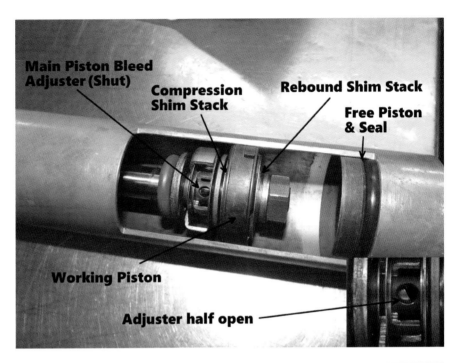

Main Piston Bleed Adjuster (Shut)

Compression Shim Stack

Rebound Shim Stack

Free Piston & Seal

Working Piston

Adjuster half open

Koni sport top adjuster – influence over rebound force.

When looking at strut-type applications, the majority of twin-tube offerings from such as Spax, Gaz and AVO have a top adjustment for rebound only. This is because the base adjuster can't be utilized due to the strut casing. In the top adjustable twin-tube strut the piston rod is hollow and the adjuster affects the rebound circuit. Mono-tube struts will tend to have an adjuster either on the top of the damper (hollow piston rod – this affects bump and rebound) or if they are inverted struts, the adjuster will generally be underneath.

Bilstein B16 base adjuster – influence over rebound and compression.

DOUBLE ADJUSTABLE DAMPER

A double adjustable damper will have a separate circuit for compression and rebound. There are a number of different ways of achieving this. With a typical mono-tube damper the adjuster will need to be on both sides of the piston. There will usually be two inline rotary adjusters.

The ability to adjust the compression and rebound circuits independently makes it possible to tune the damper to the vehicle chassis much more easily. With single adjustment, in practice you will tend to use the damper, once set, to add or lose grip at the end of the chassis that has too much grip. For example, if a front-wheel-drive car is understeering you can turn up the rear damper for compression and rebound to make the rear more mobile.

With a double adjuster, much greater possibility for tuning exists. For example, consider a vehicle braking hard for a tight corner. In this situation, let us imagine the vehicle is diving too much at the front and lifting too much at the rear. Adding front compression damping will reduce the dive. Conversely, adding rear rebound force will reduce the lift on the rear axle. Considering corner exit for a moment, if a rear-wheel-drive vehicle were suffering from traction problems coming out of the corner, it would be helpful to reduce front rebound force, and reduce rear compression force. Together these adjustments would enable faster weight transfer to the rear axle, improving traction.

The majority of double adjustable dampers predominantly affect compression and rebound in the low speed (piston velocity) area.

THREE-WAY ADJUSTABLE DAMPER

The addition of a third adjustment to the damper usually comes in the form of high speed compression. High velocity events, such as taking a kerb on a racetrack at high speed, or indeed hitting the other side of a pothole (a pothole is actually a very rapid extension event followed by a brutal compression event, often damaging the wheel due to the acute angles and damper forces involved), can be tuned with a three-way damper.

Penske two-way adjuster (rebound and compression independently).

Bilstein two-way adjuster.

Anti-roll Bars

The purpose of an anti-roll bar (*aka* sway bar) is to reduce body roll whilst cornering. As a vehicle rounds a corner, weight is transferred via the sprung mass. The amount of weight transfer is a function of the centre of gravity (CG) height and the track width. As you can imagine, a low and wide vehicle such as a formula racing car will have less weight transfer than a tall, narrow vehicle. Anti-roll bars don't have much effect on the overall amount of weight transfer, but they do control the proportion of it from front to rear, and they successfully control body roll.

The first anti-roll bar patent was lodged by Canadian inventor Stephen Coleman in 1919. A typical anti-roll bar will be shaped like a wide letter 'U'. As you can see from the image, the bar is connecting both sides of the suspension. In operation the bar now resists the vehicle's tendency to roll via its springs.

The stiffness of an anti-roll bar is a function of the material used, the fourth power of its radius, and the inverse of the length of the arms. The fourth power of the radius clearly makes a 1mm change in bar thickness very noticeable. The stiffest possible anti-roll bar for a given size would have no arms. Conversely, long levers will significantly reduce the stiffness. The geometry and stiffness of the mounting points is

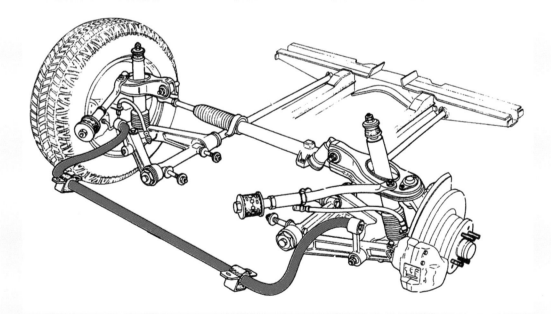

The location of an anti-roll bar (in red).

$$K \text{ (lbs/in)} = \frac{500,000 \, (OD^4 - ID^4)}{(0.4244 \times A^2 \times B) + (0.2264 \times C^3)}$$

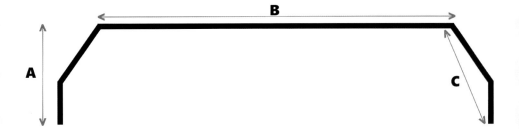

Anti-roll bar stiffness calculator.

also a factor. For example, the bar could be solidly mounted to a semi-independent trailing arm suspension, or it could be mounted via brackets and bushes and drop links.

The stiffer the bar, the greater the force required to move left and right wheels in relation to each other. Although the suspension springs also resist roll, the amount of roll stiffness they can offer is extremely low compared to an anti-roll bar. Providing useful roll stiffness using springs alone would result in a back-breaking ride.

Calculating the exact amount of roll stiffness that a specific anti-roll bar will give would require an extremely complex formula. Fortunately a number of writers and engineers have sought to simplify the calculation. A popular formula, which is usually very accurate, was created by Fred Puhn. This is widely used as it simplifies the formula so you only need a few basic dimensions. The formula is shown in the picture above.

The output K is in lb/inch, and all the other inputs should be inches.

Enabling the vehicle to ride kerbs on a racetrack can make it much faster over the course of a lap. In addition, it provides added options for overtaking on track. It is rare you will see drivers specifying three-way dampers for a road car, but understanding their benefits in tuning the vehicle chassis to engage with, but not be bullied by, the road surface means they are not wasted on a road car, particularly in a country with many bad roads. Witness the Renault Clio's Trophy variant, which utilized a three-way damper, albeit with the adjustment locked out, to avoid the calamity of operator error and lawsuits.

A three-way damper will usually have the high speed and low speed compression adjustment on the remote canister. This will be an auxiliary reservoir of oil (and gas on mono-tubes) with its own piston and shim stack. The high speed adjustment is activated only on high velocity damper movements.

FOUR-WAY ADJUSTABLE DAMPER

The most common adjustment to add with a four-way damper is to split the rebound circuit into high and low speed. With dampers, it is again worth stating that this speed is not in relation to the vehicle speed. With the rebound circuit, we are dealing with the energy stored in the spring. Movements of the vehicle around a corner occur at a low frequency, and these would be affected by the low speed adjustment. High levels of low speed rebound will prevent roll by slowing the extension of the inside damper (on the opposite wheel it is compression damping that slows the upward movement of the wheel). Whilst low speed rebound damping is useful for controlling roll, if there is too much force it will prevent the tyre from pushing back down into the surface.

HYDRO-PNEUMATIC SUSPENSION

Hydro-pneumatic suspension was invented by Frenchman Paul Magès. A particularly interesting aspect of this incredible invention was that Magès didn't have the kind of educational background you would expect for this level of automotive engineering. After gaining his national diploma at seventeen years old, he sent his CV to Citroën. Starting in 1925 at a fairly low level within the organization, requisite of his age and experience, by 1936 he had progressed into technical drafting, and then in 1942 the CEO promoted him to the development department. Here he specialized in braking and suspension systems.

It is said that Magès' lack of technical training may have been part of the reason for his innovative thinking. A French playwright called Marcel Pagnol once said: 'Everyone thought it was impossible, except an idiot who didn't know and who created it.' Almost bizarrely, Magès kept a copy of this statement on his desk. In Britain we love the underdog, and that is what makes this invention uniquely appealing.

The brief for the design called for a system that provided fast travel on poor road surfaces, and Magès' invention achieved this spectacularly well. If you've never been in a Citroën with hydro-pneumatic suspension, you really should try one. The way the vehicle glides over bumps in the road and maintains a level posture no matter what humps arrive, is nothing short of amazing. The author remembers marvelling at the system in a Citroën C5 during a taxi ride back from a wedding. With his tongue loosened by alcohol, he waxed lyrical about it, and the driver, seemingly flattered, responded to the praise by driving faster and faster.

MAGÈS' SYSTEM EXPLAINED

The system that Magès designed utilizes two technological principles. A pneumatic spring works on the principle that a gas is compressible, and at higher pressures, the spring is effectively stiffer. This means that the system automatically compensates for greater load. The second principle is that hydraulic systems using a liquid that isn't compressible, offer the ability both to damp a spring and supply torque multiplication. Damping we have covered in the previous section; torque multiplication means that force can be applied to any corner of the car, without cause for gears or levers.

What this means in practice is that the majority of systems can offer both self-levelling and a variation in ride height, either adjusted by the driver, or chosen by the firmware on the control system (the latest systems are computer controlled, while early systems are simply mechanical).

If it were possible to insert a video into this book at this point, most helpful would be an episode of the popular motoring show where they sought to see if the latest Citroën C6 model still had what it took to be a stable camera platform on a racecourse, something the old DS had done before. When we say 'racecourse' we are talking horses, and typically the kind of surface that would send a spring- and shock-equipped car into a round of frenzied pitching reminiscent of a bucking bronco. They compare the Citroën with a current model BMW, and are telling how hopeless the spring- and shock-equipped BMW is at this task. Were it not for the fact that hydro-pneumatic systems add significant cost, it is very likely that their use would have been much more widespread.

HOW THE CITROËN SYSTEM WORKS

In the image you can see the suspension sphere. The sphere has a flexible diaphragm seal separating the upper and lower hemispheres. In the upper hemisphere, the sphere is filled with stable nitrogen gas; in the lower hemisphere a specialist hydraulic fluid is used. This started out as brake fluid and then progressed through a number of different grades (see section below).

As the vehicle wheel traverses the road surface, the piston at the bottom of the hydraulic circuit moves up and down. The hydraulic fluid acting on the gas above provides the equivalent of a suspension spring. Damping of this spring is provided by the fluid, which must make its way backwards and forwards through a leaf-type valve. Raising the system pressure is achieved by increasing the volume of fluid in

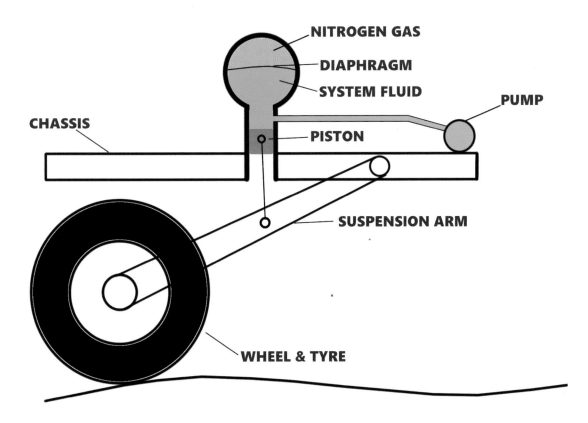

Citroën hydro-pneumatic suspension system.

Citroën CX 1974: hydro-pneumatic suspension in raised height mode.

the sphere. This pressurizes the gas, which therefore increases the spring rate. The range of operation is wide enough for the vehicle to sit extremely low when switched off, and then rise when the engine is started and the hydraulic pump begins.

The ride height is controlled by valves connected to the anti-roll bars. These valves are only in operation to set the static ride height. If a fault develops the vehicle will either sit too low or too high.

There are usually five or six spheres: those with five have one for each wheel and one main accumulator, while those with six have a dedicated brake accumulator. The latest systems, known as hydractive, have up to ten spheres, because as well as controlling pitch, they also act on yaw and roll.

The real beauty of the system is its ability to keep the car flat so that it doesn't suffer from pitching. When a regular car suspension hits a hump in the road, the front of the vehicle is moved upwards, while the rear waits for the same bump. Depending on the length of the wheelbase, the time taken before the rear hits the same bump will vary. Quite quickly, though, on a very uneven surface, the car will start to feel like a ship at sea. It is possible to pitch optimize a regular spring-suspended car for a given speed by making the rear suspension stiffer than the front. This does, however, have some negative consequences for ride quality, and above or below the optimized speed the chassis is not working as effectively.

The Citroën system controls pitch by manipulating the pressure on the other axle. With more spheres and electronic control the system is also able to control yaw and roll.

The System Fluid

Originally the system fluid used was standard brake fluid, but Citroën developed this into a red fluid known as LHS. This was glycol based, like brake fluid, and as such was hygroscopic (it attracted water). However, in order that the system could raise and lower the vehicle, it was not sealed to the atmosphere. This meant that as system pressure was raised by increas-

An old can of LHS used for models from 1954 to 1967.

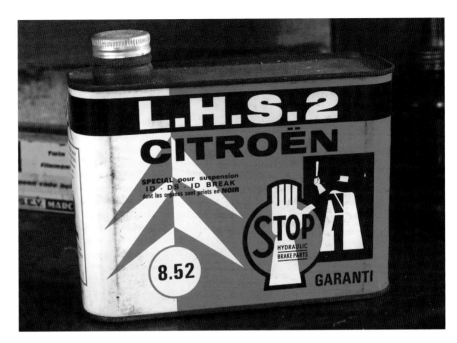

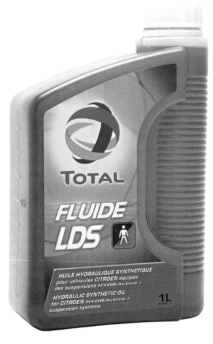

LHM green for 1967 to 2001, and LDS for hydractive 3 – the Citroën C5 from 2001 and on.

ing the volume of fluid in the sphere, the suspension would rise, and the volume of fluid in the reservoir would fall. At the same time this would draw in air from the atmosphere. As we know, depending on the climate, a varying amount of water vapour will be present in the atmosphere, and because this was absorbed by the early LHS fluid, it led to corrosion of mechanical parts.

Citroën later developed LHM fluid, which is mineral-based oil – the kind of fluid you could run in the gearbox. This was coloured green, and solved the water-absorption issue. Of course, along with air and moisture, there are particulates, which will be unwelcome in the system. Therefore, in the same way that a combustion engine is equipped with an oil filter and an air filter to keep the internals clean, so is the Citroën hydraulic system. The latest systems use an orange-coloured fluid called LDS, which is designed for longer life. Just like oil changes for a car engine, long life and reliable performance go hand-in-hand with regular oil and filter changes.

It is also vital to ensure that as well as regular changes, the correct grade of fluid is used.

THE HYDRACTIVE SYSTEM

The original hydro-pneumatic design was developed into a much more sophisticated system, first seen on the Citroën Activa concept in 1988, and introduced into their production models in 1990.

Sensors on the steering, suspension, brakes, accelerator and gearbox provide real-time information of the car's speed and acceleration, as well as cornering forces. This data is fed to a central processing unit, which is able to rapidly – within milliseconds – engage or disengage secondary spheres, which can change the ride comfort, and even roll resistance. Equipped with this suspension, the Xantia will corner flat right up to the limit of the tyres' adhesion.

As well as making the car comfortable on the inside (body roll is rarely well received by occupants) this suspension has the secondary benefit of optimizing tyre contact patch. Through extension and compression, most suspension designs will see some significant camber change, which can often lose grip on the limit. However, the Xantia was able to achieve peak G data beyond what you'd expect with the standard hydro-pneumatic system, or indeed a conventionally sprung system.

Various iterations of the hydractive system have appeared over the years; the Hydractive 3+ was the pinnacle of the development, the system measuring data from the following:

- vehicle speed
- ride height, both front and rear
- steering-wheel angle/speed sensor
- longitudinal G
- lateral G
- body movement

Using this data it is possible for the hydractive ECU not only to influence pitch, yaw and roll, but to do it with a different overall mode. So for example in sport mode, the suspension will elect to have much stiffer roll control than it would in comfort mode. The system would assume the driver is much more willing to lose out on comfort in return for more outright grip. Conversely in normal and comfort operation modes the system will have less roll resistance and more suspension movement, enabling the vehicle to 'glide' over the surface of the road. This system is truly active suspension.

It is powerful technology, so much so that it has been used under licence by various manufacturers. Maserati was an early user, partly because of ownership by Citroen at the time. Rolls-Royce used the technology to achieve a magic carpet ride. In more recent times, award-winning adverts by Mercedes-Benz have sought to liken the suspension performance of their cars to the way a chicken naturally adjusts its orientation: the adverts show that even as the chicken's body is moved around, its head stays still. The Mercedes version of the Citroën system is actually known as Active Body Control – however, 'Chicken Ride' is arguably catchier.

Most car engineers would argue that truly active suspension systems bring significant benefits to the table. We have seen that Citroën have really nailed the system, and that other notable manufacturers use it under licence. So why isn't it more widespread? In essence it is the age-old issue of cost. Car manufacturers exist to make a profit for themselves or their shareholders, and the complexity of an active suspension system puts significant additional cost into a vehicle. Most cars are sold into a competitive market segment, and whilst adding obvious technology such as significant horsepower and performance is usually easy to sell, unfortunately suspension systems are not. Usually a short test drive of a vehicle will have the driver concentrating on lots of different elements. Although they may well pick up on the ride quality, they are rarely concerned with ride comfort on such a short drive. Equally it is unlikely they will be trying to generate more than 1G around corners on a test drive on the road.

So this is why, in many instances, the hydro-pneumatic suspension system is one that you only notice and learn to love when you live with it, when you've had time to drive the car on a wide range of roads. But this doesn't help the carmaker sell it on a car – unless perhaps it is a luxury car: witness Maserati, Mercedes-Benz and Rolls-Royce being licensees, and it is easy to see why this is the case. This is perhaps why manufacturers nowadays often offer a twenty-four-hour test drive to let the car get under the driver's skin.

THE FUTURE FOR CITROËN'S HYDRACTIVE SYSTEM

Many current Citroën models are conventionally sprung, and it seems that with their latest 'invention' perhaps they are trying to phase out the hydrac-tive system altogether. Citroën's latest Advanced Comfort® programme has delivered the system known as Progressive Hydraulic Cushions®.

This is a much simpler system, and if anything, is brought about by the pressure on margins in the sector in which Citroën operates. The Progressive Hydraulic Cushions® enable the car to be softly sprung, and control large movements much better than a conventional bump stop, which gives back the energy and results in uncomfortable bucking motions. Although a fairly notable journalist seemed to think this system was good, in the same breath he then complained about too much pitch in both acceleration and braking.

This points to the fact that ultimately it is a passive system, and therefore there will always be a compromise between ride and handling. But it seems rather sad that after being such a pioneer of active suspension, Citroën should end up using a technologically inferior solution in their quest to further their well established reputation for ride quality.

Citroën C4 Cactus, with a conventional suspension with hydraulic bump stops. Citroën have finally called time on their hydro-pneumatic system in production cars.

THE BMC HYDROLASTIC SYSTEM

Around the same time that Citroën were developing their hydro-pneumatic design, Alex Moulton invented the hydrolastic suspension system. This was a simpler design than the Citroën system, but offered some similar and unique benefits.

Whereas the Citroën system relied on air for the springs, Moulton, being the famous rubber engineer that he was, used that material to good effect and replaced steel springs with rubber cones. Covered earlier in this chapter, we have seen that rubber lends a few unique qualities to a suspension, namely rising rate on force deflection, as well as high hysteresis (reducing the need for damping).

A hydrolastic system features displacer units that are fluid filled and contain a rubber spring. Damping is achieved by rubber valves that restrict the flow of fluid through them.

What is really clever is that the front and rear units are interconnected as a left and right pair. When the fluid is displaced by a load on the wheel (for example, when a hitting a bump), displaced fluid moves to the opposing unit on the other axle. This allows the vehicle to remain composed in pitch over uneven surfaces.

THE BMC HYDRAGAS SYSTEM

Hydragas was the next evolution in BMC's attempt at solving conventional suspension's biggest weakness. Gone were the rubber springs, which were replaced by a pressurized sphere containing nitrogen gas. Each sphere is separated by a diaphragm from the underside, which was filled with hydraulic fluid. Pressurizing the hydraulic fluid increases the pressure of the nitrogen in the sphere. The car is 'pumped up' to a specific pressure dictated by a ride-height figure. The units are hermetically sealed and theoretically should last a lifetime – although hydragas pump-ups are still an ongoing service requirement, as some fluid loss over time is likely. Unfortunately the gas cannot be replaced, so eventually the car ends up with more liquid and less gas and too firm a ride, necessitating replacement hydragas units.

Damping is provided by valves within the hydraulic system, and the spheres are interconnected from front to rear. The system is remarkably similar to Citroën's, but it has a fixed system pressure, and it is sealed to the atmosphere. So the BMC system is technically maintenance free, without the need for fluid and filter changes.

Of course without the pump and fluid capacity of the Citroën design, it is not possible for the vehicle to make changes in ride height. Neither did this system receive the long-term development of the Citroën system. Therefore it was always passive, and never received the kind of electronic control that made the Citroën system so startling in its later iterations.

The death knell of the hydragas system came when the makers BTR increased the price considerably, prompting Rover to switch to conventional suspension. What could have happened if the system had been properly developed? Perhaps Rover would still be alive today, making smooth riding, good handling, good looking, economical cars with a sense of understated style. Their *pièce de résistance* could have been a suspension system of supple riding, but of relatively low maintenance and cost. Actively controlled perhaps Rover could have made 'best in class' every time. Alas it was not to be, and ultimately the end was caused by pimping up models such as MGs without any true innovation. There was the threat of a Phoenix Rising as the fastest car on track at a wet Le Mans, but the car's electrics hadn't been designed to work in pools of water *inside* the car. So it was a brief flash of hope before the brand was decimated by bad management and a lack of funds.

If you get a chance to drive a well maintained hydragas-equipped car (this is getting harder now), you will appreciate how, over large road imperfections, the car remains composed and doesn't pitch.

MCLAREN AND THE TENNECO KINETIC SYSTEM

When looking at the Rover system you may recall that the price increase from the supplier BTR saw the end of the hydragas system in production Rover cars. It is notable at this point because this was a third-party supplier. The cars Rover were making were very much mainstream at a mid-range price band, and they couldn't justify the expense. However, if you are designing a supercar then you have a very different target market, one that expects the absolute pinnacle of performance.

The reality of supercars, at the time of writing, is that most are equipped with some kind of electronic suspension control. However, most of the time the control elements involve simply changing damping response, and the majority of supercars are still equipped with springs and anti-roll bars.

When McLaren launched the 12C supercar, they employed some game-changing semi-active suspensions. Just as Rover had used an external supplier, McLaren turned to Tenneco, well known for its Monroe brand. It is rare that car makers will try to do everything in house, and once again this helps us appreciate the significance of the Citroën system.

Utilizing the Kinetic system from Tenneco, the most notable difference between the 12C and its competition was the lack of anti-roll bars. Anti-roll bars control the body roll that most cars experience when cornering. They fairly crudely interconnect left and right sides with a piece of sprung steel. The 12C instead employed hydraulic anti-roll bars. The dampers were interconnected from left to right, and if you are familiar with wiring a loudspeaker, they were essentially wired in series. So just as the negative would be connected to the positive, the compression circuit on one side was connected to the rebound circuit on the other.

What this means is the car can resist roll by moving hydraulic fluid, with the assistance of a high-pressure pump. So as the car rounds a right-hander, sensors detect the g-force on the left-hand side of the car, and the hydraulic system is programmed to provide an amount of rebound force to the right-hand side. In order to give the driver some kind of feedback there is a certain amount of roll, but it is significantly less than you'd experience with conventional anti-roll bars. The real benefit is that without connecting both sides of the suspension together permanently, ride quality over single wheel bumps isn't worsened. Theoretically you could prevent roll with big anti-

roll bars, but the ride and traction would suffer as a result.

In addition the system on the 12C interconnects the dampers both front and rear, and as a result, can also control pitch and provide variable modes for more or less compliance in the suspension. Experiencing a passenger ride in this vehicle, it is initially difficult to think about suspension due to the brutally fast acceleration and serious stopping power. Quite quickly, though, you start to realize how supple the ride is. It deploys devastating power and torque with very little fuss, and in comfort mode rides over bumps almost as if they weren't there.

Despite this, the 12C system is still only semi-active – it still doesn't change the ride height or the spring rate. You will need to look at the P1 and Senna for the full system. The 12C system has four accumulators (similar to the Citroën Spheres), but the body is still suspended on steel springs. In the P1 and Senna only around one third of the bodyweight is suspended on the springs. It has eight accumulators, enabling the vehicle to vary ride height as well as spring rate.

To all intents and purposes this system operates in a similar manner to the Citroën hydractive system, the key difference being that springs are still present. It is marketed by Tenneco as 'Acocar', and is their top-of-the-range system designed for use in high-end automobiles. It will be interesting to see if others follow McLaren's lead, or if they keep to conventional springs and active dampers.

THE FUTURE FOR HYDRO-PNEUMATIC SYSTEMS

Conventional sprung cars with passive hydraulic dampers still make up the majority of the car park. However, with autonomous vehicles just around the corner, and the seemingly insatiable appetite for incongruous SUVs, ride quality is becoming more of a focus than ever. Prior to this, safety was probably the key concern – and before this, arguably the heyday of the motorcar, performance and styling were king. So it looks as if finally, active suspension could gain the market penetration that it has always threatened to. More widespread adoption of the systems will bring the price down. It is likely that in the not-too-distant future suspension systems will be able to give the owner two cars in one. This, and a drive for greater efficiency, will probably see the modern car park unrecognizable from what we have today, with sleek, lightweight, aerodynamic cars that can drive both off road and on road. If the user wants a lofty driving position he need only press a button, rather than resort to a car that is permanently high off the ground.

McLaren have shown the way this system can work in a sports car, and we are highly likely to see it filtered down to more basic models soon. The complexity of settings available means there is likely to be a new growth market for suspension system remapping.

Tenneco seem to have their bases covered for any direction the market may take, producing a range of solutions below Acocar and Kinetic which focus on various flavours of CVSA – continuously variable semi-active suspension. The more basic versions don't include roll control. Then they move down to DRIV technology, which incorporates a triple tube damper with an external electronically controllable valve, which enables them to overcome the disadvantages of traditional shim stacks. Next on the menu is simply widely adjustable damping across a range of curves. Its most basic offering is a dual mode adjustable damper.

Much more detail is given to damping in the book, so those systems will be looked at in more detail. Safe to say there is passive suspension, passive damping, active suspension and active damping, and a range of combinations between. It's nothing like the war between VHS and Betamax, but the real test will be to see if the predominantly active systems can penetrate the market in the future. Paul Magès would almost certainly think so.

ACTIVE SUSPENSION

In the section on hydro-pneumatic suspension, some comment was made of the various active systems that came to be. Interestingly, when you study the Citroën hydro-pneumatic system, it is very apparent that ride quality was always the primary concern. Arguably even when they developed the Xantia Activa, the market never really perceived Citroën as a developer of vehicles with high performance handling, so it is useful to look at how active suspension developed in the sphere of motor sport.

Before we start this, it is important to emphasize that a truly active suspension system is a rare thing. Unless the central processing unit is given free rein in control of the wheel, then a system can never be truly active. Only by allowing change in spring rate, damping control, yaw, pitch and roll in accordance with a central processing unit logic array, is a system truly active. So for example Citroën's Hydractive 2 is technically semi-active, but Hydractive 3 is fully active. This is a fairly ambiguous point, however, as evidenced by the 1990 Infiniti Q45 'Full-Active Suspension (FAS)', an active suspension system that still had the car on conventional coil springs. In this case, are we really going to argue that the McLaren P1 doesn't have truly active suspension due to the use of coil springs?

Readers of this book are probably aware that in all FIA-governed motor-sport events, some form of suspension is required, generally speaking in the form of springs and dampers. However, it wasn't always this way: active suspension was fully adopted in Formula One, and was then promptly banned. As a fan of suspension this does seem somewhat odd, when the sport allows complicated hybrid systems, but prohibits active suspension.

Lotus led the way with active suspension design. Unlike the earlier passive Citroën systems, this system uses hydraulic rams instead of gas for springing, and features computer-controlled valves which enable extremely fine adjustments to be made almost instantaneously. This effectively created a damper that was also a spring at the same time. In terms of rate the spring could clearly be infinitely variable, from soft to locked solid.

Springs in a road car are designed to create comfort. For racing, much stiffer springs are required – in fact in Formula One the cars were getting stiffer and stiffer, since aerodynamic developments had necessitated a stiff spring. In addition there was the age-old problem of camber control. Engineers therefore just decided to run the cars as stiff as a board, and although it was uncomfortable for the drivers, it worked.

This is why active suspension took a while to show true promise. For example, if you were to bring active suspension into karting, it would probably take you many years to get an advantage to override the additional weight and complexity. So the task that faced Lotus was considerable, and working with computer control at the limits of available technology, they were really pioneers.

It is helpful to understand one of the benefits of active suspension when you consider the problem that it set out to solve. The Lotus 80 was generating nearly all of its downforce from ground effects. However, what the conventional springs were doing, was resonating in pitch. That would then change the height of the vehicle, which would then change the available downforce. It was sometimes known as porpoising. Surely they just needed to run it stiffer? When they tried that, it just bounced around on its tyres instead.

Lotus were provided with a solution by the aero industry, specifically from machinery designed to create feedback for the 'pilot' of a drone aircraft, where technology was developed to switch the valves ultrafast. The real skill in what they were doing was the acquisition of data, the interpretation of that data, and then the responses to that. Put this feedback into a loop, and eventually the design will come good.

Williams F1 created a similar solution, but they used an existing suspension solution and adapted it to their needs.

Automotive Products effectively created their own version of the Citroën system, for use in production cars. However, it doesn't ever seem to have worked as well as the Citroën system, nor did it see widespread adoption. But this didn't stop Frank Dernie at Williams adapting the system very successfully for use on the Williams FW11B. Lotus may have pioneered the use of active suspension, but while they were resting on their laurels and trying to

develop a system for road cars (for a time the Lotus 92 was converted back to conventional suspension), Williams grabbed hold of the idea and ran with it.

Dernie had decided that the most important principle was controlling the aerodynamic efficiency of the car. Far from trying to achieve a comfortable ride, all the effort went into developing the AP system to control the ride height effectively. The majority of the downforce was coming from the ride height and ground-effect aerodynamic forces. If this could be controlled accurately, the car could be optimized for maximum speed at all points of the circuit.

So the car was terrifically fast, but was the suspension it had actually active? Well, technically not, because it was not controlled by computer in its earliest form, nor could it apply force to any particular wheel as required.

When you initially research the Automotive Products system you discover that in the original production car arrangement, it had double-acting hydraulic struts on the rear, and single-acting on the front. This is where the only fundamental change was made by Dernie for Williams, in that they were switched around, pushing the double-acting units to the front. Apparently Dernie was fairly reticent to provide any explanation as to why. Initial thoughts turn to the fact that in a production arrangement it would be more important to control pitch, and that could be more effectively achieved by the rear axle. In the crucible of F1, on the other hand, ultimately front-end grip was king, and perhaps the active control of the front end gave a quicker lap time, which would explain why he swapped the units around.

Whatever the real reasoning for the change, the performance of the FW11B did the talking, eventually winning nine races (albeit many of these in the earlier non-active form, so it was a good car to start with!) in 1987, and taking the constructors' and drivers' championships.

In 1988 Williams ran the FW12. However, there was a design flaw in the reservoir, which wasn't discovered until much later, and this meant that the car was great for three or four laps, and then became undrivable. Due to these issues Williams didn't run active suspension in 1989, 1990 or 1991. Then in 1992, Williams created a car that was arguably more sophisticated than any Formula One car to date: the FW 14B and FW 15C. It featured active suspension, anti-lock brakes, traction control, telemetry, fly-by-wire controls, pneumatic valve springs, power steering and even automatic transmission – and as a result, Alain Prost described the car as 'a little airbus'.

Subsequently the FIA sought to ban a number of these technologies, which were seen as driver aids. Arguably anti-lock brakes and automatic transmission do weaken the visceral thrill of a Formula One car, but it seems remiss of the governing authorities to ban active suspension.

In reality it matters little how the system operates, but more about what data you obtain, and what you do with it.

ADAPTIVE SUSPENSION

The best way to think about adaptive suspension is as an active suspension 'light'. Although available from a variety of manufacturers as original equipment on a production car, there isn't a prescribed set of criteria that makes it easy to differentiate between adaptive suspension systems and devise nomenclature for them. Technically you could arrange them in the order described below.

User-adjustable damping in the cockpit: one- or two-way combined

The simplest systems from original equipment manufacturers may well be linked into a mode button such as comfort, sport or race. Usually the vehicle will have a number of other adjustments that will link into other systems, such as power steering, braking and throttle response/power delivery. The basic damping system will vary the damping via a set of motors (sometimes wired, sometimes wireless) and will probably change all four wheels at the same time.

Usually with this kind of system the changes will be quite pronounced, partly to ensure the owner can differentiate clearly between the modes. This has led to some of these modern systems being slightly contrived – for example, featuring a sport mode that is really a race mode on a car that isn't going racing

(having dampers set much closer to critical damping can work well on track but is terrible on roads), or a comfort mode that leaves the dampers so lacking in rebound control that the car body is lacking control.

User-adjustable damping in the cockpit: two-way independent

Enabling control of both compression and rebound independently will require a more complicated and expensive manufacturing process. Two-way dampers involve two sets of motor controllers, and all the requisite wiring. At the time of writing this isn't the kind of technology you will see on many cars. Consequently, if the manufacturer offers this kind of system it will tend to be on a more serious performance vehicle, and will come with many more modes to suit many more environments and driver styles. Settings will tend to be more granular, or the user may simply have full access to individual compression and rebound adjustment.

It could also feature individual wheel control, which would be particularly suited to optimizing the car's set-up for a circuit with only right-hand turns, for instance.

ECU or user-adjustable damping in the cockpit: two-way combined + accelerometer input

Adding an electronic control unit enables the car to take control – however, unless you give the ECU some data to work with, it will not be able to make any adjustments. An ECU is only as good as its programming, since adding more data streams creates larger logic tables. Computers only work with one and zero, so logic gates must be constructed, and once you add in even a single accelerometer it can be seen that the number of combinations between compression and rebound on each wheel with differing rates of load around the car is myriad.

Simple iterations will look at overall G-force, rather than trying to control the car in more degrees of motion.

ECU or user-adjustable damping in the cockpit: two-way combined + accelerometer input + speed

Taking account of speed as well G-forces enables the system to be calibrated to the greater forces that higher speeds generate. Particular reference here should be made to braking forces from high speed, as even basic cars with very little power can generate over 1G of braking quite easily. The movements of the body from turning and braking and accelerating at higher speed can feel quite different. A car that feels sharp and controlled and 'pointy' at relatively low speeds can feel unstable at high speed. Having an ECU system to control damping as changing road and vehicle conditions take their toll, can make the driver's job much easier. Later on, when we look at what is involved with changing the internals of dampers, you may wonder why more of these systems don't sell. The answer is probably that many people prefer a simple solution.

TEIN EDFC ACTIVE PRO: AUTOMATICALLY ADJUSTABLE DAMPING

TEIN are a Japanese company with a proud history of suspension design and innovation at the highest levels. Arguably they pioneered aftermarket adaptive damping systems. Using a control unit and stepper motors that adjust the hydraulic valve on the damper, they are able to offer a suspension experience to

cars that considerably exceeds the majority of OEM systems. Depending on the age of the vehicle it is fitted to, it also offers a technology that wasn't available at the time of production. There are two systems available: EDFC Active and EDFC Pro (EDFC stands for 'electronic damping force controller').

EDFC Active adjusts front and rear damping force separately, but left and right simultaneously. With EDFC Active Pro, damping force for all four corners can be adjusted separately. This enables finer adjustment according to the road layout and conditions. This feature also works with automatic adjustment.

While EDFC Active enables automatic adjustments based on changes in acceleration/deceleration (longitudinal) G-force and vehicle speed, EDFC Active Pro adds the capability to adjust to lateral (cornering) G-force change. This feature offers the advantages of ability to suppress side rolls, to balance distribution of left/right cornering loads, and/or to increase cornering speed. In addition, understeering/oversteering can be controlled by adjusting the front/rear damping force separately.

This lateral G-actuated adjustment can be combined with longitudinal G-actuated adjustment for a

EDFC display around a left-hand corner: TEIN dampers get stiffer as the value is lower.

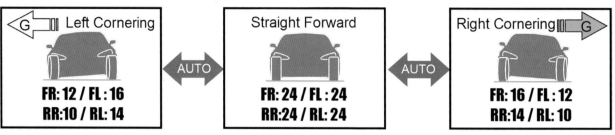

Softer Damper setting - high numbers, Harder Damper setting - lower numbers

Example of TEIN EDFC damper settings around left and right corners and straight ahead.

full 360-degree adjustment, and/or with speed-sensitive adjustment for most comprehensive adjustment. This is useful not only for improving times on tracks/circuits, but also drivability in daily use on roads.

EDFC Active Pro features a wireless control system for easy installation, and minimizes wiring. The controller unit is connected wirelessly to motor driver units, eliminating the need for troublesome wiring such as putting cables through bulkheads and/or placing/anchoring cables inside the car. This system can change each damper individually, bringing further flexibility to the set-up.

It helps to visualize how the system works from the driver's seat. Imagine you are making a left turn. In this instance weight will transfer from the left-hand side of the car to the right-hand side. Depending on the car's drive layout and characteristics, it will be possible to change the dampers on each wheel to optimize the interaction of the tyres with the tarmac. If we consider the front axle initially, the outside front damper will be dealing with a compressive force, and the inside front damper will receive an extension force. It is possible with EFDC to work with double the motors to control compression and rebound independently as well. In most installations the damper will be a single combined adjustment, however by adding EDFC, the damper adjustment granularity increases from sixteen to up to sixty-four steps. This is due to the motor's ability to rotate small amounts and hold that position.

So ideally we will increase the compression damping on the outside dampers and the rebound on the inside. However, with a single combined set-up you must always remember you are adjusting both. Moreover, increasing compression and rebound together doesn't always lead to the right result. So although your increase is usually only required in one plane, getting the other at the same time means you have to soften your adjustments. You have to compromise. The lightly loaded inside wheel, which is helping your roll control (and therefore managing the contact patch) can be increased, but not as much as the heavily loaded outside wheel. Turning up the damping too much with a combined adjuster on the heavily loaded outside wheel will result in too much rebound, which will start to result in a loss of grip.

If you consider the settings in the diagram you can see how the driven axle will need less overall damping adjustment due to the risk of a decrease in traction. These settings are clearly only a guide and each car would be unique (not least due to tyres).

So a set-up such as EDFC could easily give you an edge in competitive motor sport, though generally speaking it wouldn't be allowed. This in turn makes you question the wisdom of motor sport seeking to control set-up. The cost of an F1 car's suspension system would probably buy a number of new cars, and even for high-end single seaters the cost would be £5,000 for a set of four non-active dampers. The

TEIN EDFC system is available with a set of dampers to suit for around £1,000 to £2,000. It represents extraordinary value, and is much more useful than the typical 'sport' setting on most OEM systems.

MECHANICAL AERO SUSPENSION

At the time of writing it was prohibited in the F1 world to enable the suspension system to control the aerodynamics. However, a furore erupted because it had come to the attention of the scrutineers that some of the teams' suspension systems were facilitating a change in ride height for a given steering input. A modern Formula One car runs a complicated pushrod or pullrod suspension system, and it's not that easy to visualize how it was possible to design the suspension system to lower the car as you enter a corner.

The logic behind such a system is obvious, because as a Formula One car enters a corner, they are slowing, therefore the aerodynamic loads on the springs are reduced, and the ride height rises. This in turn worsens the aerodynamics. So if you could get a passive suspension system to lower the ride height as lock was applied, then your aerodynamics could work better, applying more 'free' aerodynamic load to the tyre, and consequentially increasing grip.

So how would you do this in practice? The way a pushrod suspension works is in principle the same as a simple MacPherson strut-type suspension. As the load is received at the wheel, movement upwards at the wheel results in compression of the spring. However, to the best of my knowledge it would not be possible to engineer this F1 system effectively with a MacPherson strut. Not that you'd want to, because the F1 car would look rather strange. However, I think it is useful to understand it by way of such a simple strut.

What they have done is offset the mounting points for the pushrod from the steering axis. What this achieves is a gradual, but increasing reduction of ride height as steering lock is applied. The offset mounting of the pushrod in relation to the steering axis essentially reduces the length of the rod. Going back to our MacPherson strut for a moment, imagine reducing the length of this strut in real time as the steering is turned. If you reduce the length of the strut the car will get lower.

So what's the big deal? Is it really active suspension? Or just a quirk of geometry? At the time of writing the FIA have decided to allow a maximum of 5mm ride-height change on lock. Rather than effectively banning the practice, this appears to suggest that they know it's been going on, and are appeasing the team that has raised the complaint in the first place. You'll probably know that in motor sport if a team gains an advantage, all too often another will seek a rule change against them.

McLaren in particular seemed to be optimizing their car with this technology. As they had been suffering with weak power and poor qualifying, but had excellent relative race pace, it shows that engineers will always find a way of increasing performance in the face of adversity.

The reality of this situation is that the modification of ride height by steering angle is leading to faster cars and more spectacular overtaking. There has been a trend in motor sport of late, of balanced performance. This is all well and good when looking at things such as peak horsepower, standard tyres and perhaps some success ballast. However, it doesn't make sense when it prevents better engineering beating inferior engineering. It doesn't make sense when a big old Bentley is allowed by regulations to beat a Ginetta. And it also doesn't make sense if a team saddled with a poor engine finds their exceptional chassis regulated against.

CHAPTER THREE

REPAIRING SUSPENSION SYSTEMS

Generally speaking, the only end user serviceable parts of a damper are those you see on the outside – for example, replacing a bonded Bush, or repairing seized locking rings on an adjustable spring platform. However, some high-end competition dampers do permit user servicing, and we will look at those in more depth later.

Assuming that your dampers are not user serviceable, you will be returning them to the manufacturer for rebuild, repair and modification. The majority of dampers are either twin-tube or mono-tube. Both designs have similarities, but are different enough to warrant looking at a strip-down and rebuild of each type.

BILSTEIN MONO-TUBE DAMPERS

The Bilstein mono-tube design, in common with other mono-tubes, utilizes gas at very high pressure. It is vital that you don't attempt to strip these units apart without specialist equipment. Because the Bilstein unit does not have a Schrader valve to add and release gas charge, it must be disassembled on a specialist machine.

The first step after putting the damper into the machine is to depressurize the gas inside the damper. This is an upside-down design that would be used in a strut-type application. The piston inside the unit is fixed, and the large chromium tube slides over the piston, guided by low friction bearings inside the strut casing.

The internals of the damper are held in place by a circlip; once this is removed, it is then possible to degas the damper. Once the gas pressure is removed, the oil is the next thing to be collected. There are two pistons inside the mono-tube design: the working

Bilstein mono-tube damper depressurized.

piston with the shim stack, and the free piston which keeps the gas charge separate from the oil.

The free piston is the next part to come out, and then the oil will follow. The damper engineer is moving the damper through its stroke using the machine to achieve this.

In the picture you can see the piston rod and working piston removed, resting on the free piston.

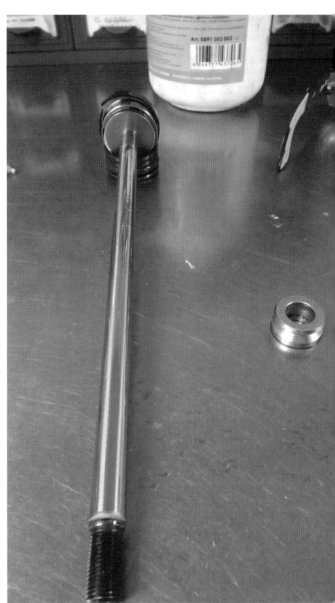

Once the gas is removed, the floating piston can be extracted and the oil removed.

Piston rod removed, working piston sat on top of the free piston.

The next step is to use the aluminium clamp to hold the piston and valve. This part is specially designed to ensure that the rod is not damaged. Once the rod is secure, the retaining nut is undone.

With the retaining nut undone, the rebound shim stack is visible. The port is on the other side, and the shims change the rate of flow through the piston.

You can see the shims are arranged in a tower-like fashion. Removing the rebound shims allows us to see the piston. You can see how the shims control the flow coming from the other side of the piston. You can also see that a different compressive stack would have an impact on the rebound flow.

With the piston removed it is now possible to see the compression shim stack.

Piston and shimstack placed in an aluminium clamp to undo the retaining nut.

With the retaining nut removed, the rebound shim stack is visible.

With the rebound shims removed, the piston is now visible.

With the piston removed, the compression shim stack is visible.

Linear (left) and digressive pistons (right) – rebound side.

Linear (left) and digressive pistons (right) – compression side.

Different piston designs give different damping curves. A linear piston will have a damping rate that consistently increases with velocity: on a graph this would be a straight line upwards. A digressive piston, on the other hand, has a greater damping response at lower speeds, which then progressively bleeds off as the rate rises – most of the time. If your unit is just being serviced, it will go back together exactly the way it came apart. However, just suppose you were getting a set of dampers changed in specification from road to rallycross. Greater loads from rally-cross would mean a linear valve would be needed to prevent the damper closing fully too easily. So when a service is being done, it is always best to consider if there are any other changes that should be made. When you have your units modified, make sure you keep details of what was changed.

In the following pictures you can see the difference between a linear and a digressive piston on both sides of the piston.

Prototype shim-stack worksheet.

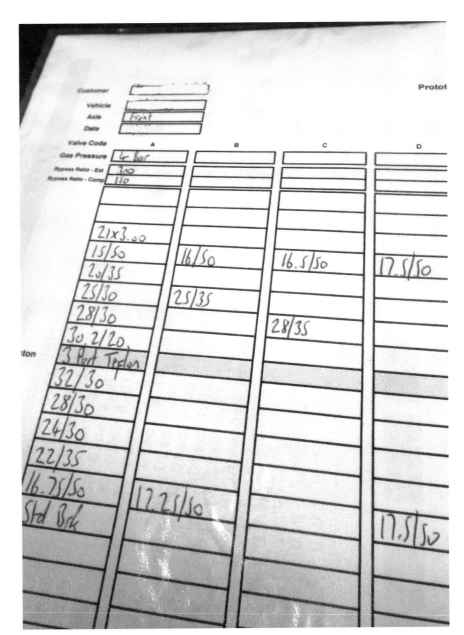

SHIM-STACK WORKSHEET

This particular unit was being modified, and you can see the worksheet the engineer was using in the picture above. This shows the shim stacks on either side of the piston. You can see the measurements for each shim, the first thing is the diameter and the second figure is the thickness in tenths of a millimetre. So for example, 28/35 is 28mm diameter and 0.35mm thickness.

The real skill in this process is providing a damper to suit the customer's requirements. The engineer will consider what the customer needs the damper for, and will use the right piston and shim stack to give the required damping response. However, this is a complicated process, and many different pistons and valves have come into being as a result – these are discussed in the following chapter, 'Modifying a Suspension System'.

Compression shim-stack ready to assemble.

Adding the compression shim stack.

The shim-stack worksheet shows an entry for axle so as to prevent confusion; it also shows an entry for gas pressure. Different gas pressures are used depending on the application and the design of the damper. Larger working areas of gas and heavier loads require higher pressures. Bilstein publish many of their motor-sport damper rates online. They quote 'Nm x 10', so it is worth bearing that in mind.

The shim stack is laid out logically as it will appear when in contact with the piston.

The compression shim stack ready to go on – you can see easily why the word 'stack' is used to describe the shims.

The shims are then checked and added to the rod, followed by the working piston. These are now in place ready for the retaining nut. The next

Free piston.

step is to insert the piston rod assembly into the sliding tube.

The piston rod is now in place ready for the measured volume of oil to be added, followed by the free piston, and then nitrogen gas. The volume and pressure of gas can be varied depending on the application.

The free piston's job is to keep the oil and gas separate. In fact it is remarkable how well this works, because you might expect the gas to pass the seal as it is under such high pressure. However, there is some science at work that makes it possible – in a way it is similar to the trick of applying a single ply of tissue paper to a bottle filled with water and being able to turn it upside down whilst full – and not a drop will spill. The air pressure acting on the single ply of tissue applies force to stop the water moving out; in a similar way the high gas pressure in a mono-tube damper prevents the oil moving past the piston.

The principle relies on the formation of a boundary layer. The same principle occurs in a combustion engine, where the boundary layer between the piston and the combustion gases prevents the piston melting. A startling example is when you consider that the safe exhaust gas temperature in a petrol engine is around 950°C, but that aluminium has a melting point of just 660°C. At the point of the

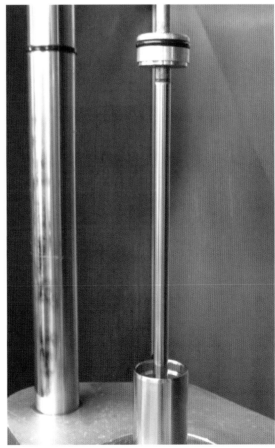

Piston rod in place ready for oil and gas.

Just a single ply of tissue paper will prevent the water escaping.

boundary layer a pressure gradient is encountered that opposes its flow, and it slows down. If this gradient is strong enough, it stops entirely and starts to form a small zone of slowly recirculating fluid and gas.

It is this principle that enables the high gas pressure mono-tube to be reliable over millions of cycles.

Specialist hydraulic oil is now added to the damper tube. Then after the free piston is inserted, nitrogen gas is added. The working pressure of the damper gas will vary depending on a number of factors, including the volume of the gas and the size of the piston. Typically, though, it will be as high as 10bar. However, the unique design of the Bilstein machine means that the gas is added as the damper is being assembled. It is then compressed before being sealed. This means the gas is usually only required at around 2–4bar pressurization, as the pressure will increase as the damper is compressed and sealed.

Oil added to the damper tube.

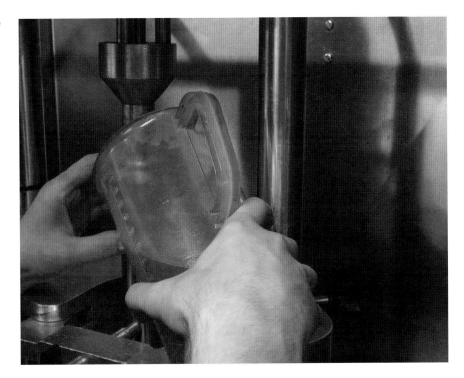

Nitrogen gas pressure is added.

SUSPENSION SPRINGS

Suspension springs are not repairable. If a spring sags or breaks it must be replaced. Generally speaking springs have a long service life and are easily sourced for replacement when necessary. Due to the metallurgy of spring steel they cannot successfully be welded to repair.

SUSPENSION ARMS

The suspension arm itself does not tend to wear – it is the bushings and ball joints on the arms that wear.

Jaguar upper control arm showing severe wear to bushes and ball joints.

Close-up of Jaguar control-arm bush (which in this case is actually a bearing with a dustboot) showing the dustboot split.

Close-up of Jaguar control-arm ball joint showing the dustboot split.

SUSPENSION BUSHES

Suspension bushes are heavily loaded components and have a key job to play in keeping the work of the suspension away from the cabin. In a racing vehicle they are often replaced by spherical bearings when noise reduction and compliance are not required. People have attempted to 'repair' bushes with a mixture of polyurethane, but this is rarely successful, as it won't bond properly to the rubber bush. You can buy aftermarket polyurethane bushes, and in some applications these can offer improved performance over a rubber item. However, there is a downside in that noise vibration and harshness (NVH) is increased. Furthermore the design of some suspension systems means the bush has to offer flexibility in one plane and resistance in another. Polyurethane bushes often struggle in this environment, adding unwanted stiffness and sometimes wearing quickly due to the lack of flexibility in the material.

INSTALLING A COIL-OVER KIT AND NEW CONTROL ARMS

After looking at damper springs, control arms and bushes individually, the following project is an installation that is quite common when trying to solve many handling issues in one hit.

TEST CAR: FIAT PANDA 100HP

When this car was introduced it was much loved by the majority of motoring journalists. For a while it seemed that Fiat had forgotten how good they were at matching a modest amount of horsepower to a responsive and engaging chassis. The Panda 100HP brought back those charms with aplomb. Arguably it harked back to the 127 Sport 70HP, and provided cheap thrills aplenty. You might doubt that being just shy of one ton and only 100HP could be much fun, but the effervescent performance of the engine and the pointy, but slightly bouncy chassis served to engage in a way that numbers cannot describe.

This particular car was still running its original dampers, which by that time were well past their

Slackening off the hub nut through the wheel centre, using an axle stand to stabilize the extension.

useful best. The 100HP was equipped with an elongated bump stop, which provided a progressively rising rear spring rate under hard cornering. Many manufacturers use expanded polyurethane foam in this way, where the bump stop is not just the last line of defence in compression, but actually an engineered part of the chassis. The downside to the bump stop coming into play is that the damper must be in good health, or some fairly severe undamped oscillations can occur.

Important note: It is a prerequisite before starting any mechanical work, particularly where lifting the chassis is involved, that the operative should have the necessary level of skill and experience.

Step 1: Remove the hub nut – optional

If you need to remove the hub nut (for example, if changing driveshafts on account of wider wishbones), be sure, if working alone, to do this through the wheel while the car is on the ground with the handbrake on. It often helps to stabilize the extension while applying torque with an axle stand.

Sometimes the wheel will need to be removed as the socket for the driveshaft won't fit through its centre, so an alternative method is to have an assistant apply the brakes, in addition to placing an axle stand underneath the hub to counteract the twisting force that you apply with a breaker bar. Driveshaft hub nuts are extremely tight and can be particularly difficult to undo as the years pass and the driveshaft starts to corrode.

In the majority of spring and damper installations it will not be necessary to remove the hub nut in order to change the suspension and control arms. In this example the Panda was being fitted with the wider wishbone from the 500, together with the longer driveshaft and different hub (it is a larger ball joint on the wider 500 wishbone).

Step 2: Jack up the vehicle safely and support it on axle stands

Would we recommend an old rusty axle stand? Well, if it is made from heavy-gauge material, it is arguably safer than a lightweight and cheaply made axle stand, resplendent in its thin coat of shiny paint. So ideally always use a stand that is well within its peak rating. What is important is that the stand makes contact with the shell in a safe way, and that the car is on level ground. Otherwise forces could make the car pull off the stand.

Sometimes you may jack up a car and see that with the handbrake on, as you jack, the car wants to move the jack and at times it looks perilous. Sometimes it is safer to jack without the handbrake on, but with the car in gear. It all depends on the car's weight, design and suspension system. The best advice in staying safe is to check the manual, and use the right tools correctly.

Secure the chassis on good quality axle stands.

Step 3: Remove the brake caliper

Whether or not the brake disc and caliper need removing to install the suspension depends on the vehicle. However, particularly when trying to fit a ball joint back into the control arm, it pays to have as little extra weight to hold on to as possible, because you will quickly tire if you can't get the ball joint back in. This is even more the case when the angles of the steering axis inclination are increased by widening the track width on a MacPherson strut suspension.

The suggestion would be to remove the brake caliper and hang it out of the way.

Step 4: Remove the brake disc

Removing the brake discs themselves can prove troublesome if the disc is 'glued' to the hub as a result of corrosion. It is no joke to say that sometimes a job can require a special level of brute force to remove particularly seized discs. Blow torches, large hammers and a great deal of determination can all be required at times.

That is, of course, if you can successfully remove the retaining screw first. It will often shear off, in which case you will need an accurate centre punch, a sharp drill and excellent technique to drill out and clean the threads with a tap. To prevent this, a tech-

Hang up the brake caliper securely out of the way.

Remove the brake disc.

nique that helps in the removal of stubborn nuts and bolts is karate. You are not trying to incapacitate the car with your strike, but if you strike it with a wrench the resulting high torque surge over a short duration often releases stubborn fastenings, without rounding off the socket or drive bit.

It is like karate in that the force you deliver can be multiplied many times by technique, focus, and of course practice. There will be some parts of a car on which you can use your human impact wrench technique to great effect. The idea is to use the smallest necessary wrench and strike, rather than a longer extension bar. If you are working on a valuable car

this tip is even more useful. Of course some nuts will need big bars, such as driveshaft nuts or crankshaft pulleys.

Step 5: Loosen (but do not remove completely) the strut to hub bolts

These bolts are likely to be well corroded, and ideally will be replaced with new bolts on reassembly. However, if you are reusing the bolts it pays to clean up the threads properly and apply releasing fluid before attempting to remove them. If a bolt shears whilst doing this, don't be too despondent, as it is quite common. Again, the technique used to remove

Loosen the strut to hub bolts.

Split the ball joint.

them is important. An impact wrench is generally very effective at undoing these nuts. If not, remember the open hand or hammer fist strike on the wrench to try and mirror the action of the impact wrench.

In the event that the vehicle has camber bolts, or larger holes to facilitate camber adjustment, it pays to mark the position before undoing the bolts.

The reason you are only loosening the bolts at this stage, and not completely removing them, is that if you remove them the hub will then be free to move around, which isn't helpful when you are trying to split the ball joint.

Step 6: Split the ball joint

Various tools are available to split a ball joint. The simplest of all is a hammer, which if brought down with enough force on to the lower arm, should see the ball joint come free from its taper. Unfortunately this technique is likely to damage the control arm, and often the ball joint still won't release. Other tools exist that will pry the joint apart, where the operator turns a bolt until there is a loud crack and the ball joint releases. Very often you will be replacing the control arm together with the ball joint, and in these cases the very simple fork-style tool works

Deteriorated ball-joint dust cover.

Fiat Panda and Fiat 500 control arm compared.

Split the steering-rod end from its taper joint.

brilliantly. Unfortunately there is a greater risk of damage to the dust cover with this tool, so either be extra careful, or use one of the bolt-operated lever-style units if you wish to reuse the ball joint.

In this Fiat Panda it is clear that the original ball-joint dust cover has had its day. The new wider wishbones from the 500 come with a new ball joint. However, this ball joint is a larger diameter, and therefore the hubs must also be changed over.

If we compare the original Fiat Panda control arm (bottom in the picture) with the Fiat 500 control arm (top), it is easy to see the extra track width that the longer arm will give. Track width and its interplay with the car's wheelbase are discussed in more depth in Chapter 4. Briefly, by widening the front track on this front-wheel-drive car, a reduction in weight transfer will occur, which, given how heavily loaded the front tyres are, should free up more overall cornering grip by making use of spare capacity in the rear tyres.

Step 7: Split the steering-rod end from its taper joint (optional)

The Panda was being fitted with 500 hubs so in this instance it was necessary to split the steering-rod end off the hub. If you were only fitting a wider wishbone and keeping the same hub you could dispense with this step.

How difficult the rod end is to remove really is anyone's guess. Sometimes a judicious tap with a hammer (wind the nyloc nut back on so you don't damage the thread) might be all that is required. The benefit of this technique is that it won't damage the dust cover. In the event that the rod end will not split, then the same tools that were used to split the ball joint can be employed.

Step 8: Undo the damper top mounting nut

The strut is close to being removed now, so take care to undo this bolt using the correct method. An impact wrench can be used, but the problem is

Undo the damper top mounting nut.

that it may spin the piston rod: this is because if the nut doesn't come undone easily, the impact wrench may find it easier to spin the damper piston rod – and if you are not careful, you can easily damage the damper. On a high-pressure mono-tube you could even remove the retaining nut of the working piston and cause the assembly to burst apart.

The majority of strut-type dampers have an allen key way-machined into the pin, and that should be used to stabilize the piston rod whilst the nut is undone. Don't make the mistake of trying to undo the nut by applying force to the allen bolt, just use that to stabilize your effort on the large nut. Ideally it helps to have an assistant to hold one wrench while you try to undo the top nut. The logic here is that the allen head is fairly small, and the process of using a rachet on it puts more local load and wear into the smaller fitting. Ideally if you have it, a rachet ring spanner for the larger nut will be the easiest option.

Step 9: Remove the strut and spring assembly

Another good reason for having an assistant at hand for this operation is that as you undo the top nut the strut can suddenly drop down. Therefore take hold of the strut assembly as the top mounting nut is undone, and remove it carefully from the wing aperture, taking care not to knock the paintwork on the edge of the wing. This warning might seem obvious, but it is surprising how little room there is with the hub and driveshaft in place – and of course the more expensive the car, the more careful you need to be.

Step 10: Remove the hub (if it is being changed)

When a driveshaft is removed from the gearbox, oil may come out. If it doesn't, it means that either you have remembered to drain the box, or you forgot and the box has been running very low on oil. It is often surprising how much gearboxes are neglected with regard to routine maintenance. However, more modern gearboxes, particularly the DSG style from Volkswagen, have proved more problematic. They have specific service requirements, often due to the use of wet clutches, so make sure you adhere to the schedule on this type of box. But regardless of the style of gearbox, changing the oil usually helps with shift quality.

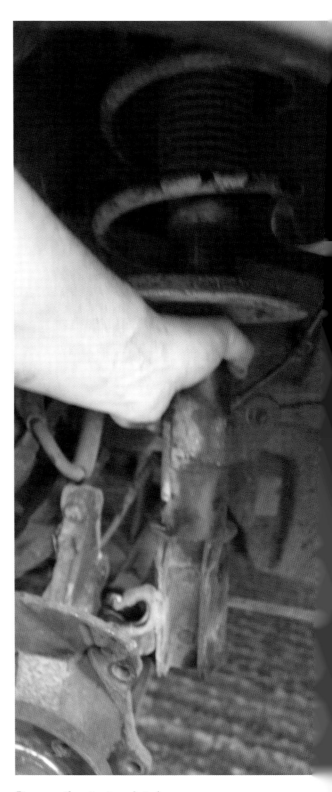

Remove the strut and spring.

Tap the driveshaft to ease its removal from the hub.

Removing the hub from the driveshaft.

Make sure you completely drain the oil first, and afterwards replace it with the correct grade. Using a suitable drift, tap the end of the shaft: unless the splines have heavily rusted into the hub, this part should come away fairly easily. On the rare occasion where significant corrosion has occurred (perhaps because of salt water, or because it is a very old, neglected car) then it might be best to remove the hub and driveshaft to the workbench.

Step 11: Compressing the spring

Place the strut assembly on a stable surface. If you are working outside when the weather is warm, an inexpensive DIY-style folding workbench is ideal. The gap that can be set in the middle of the two boards allows positive location of the spring and damper assembly.

Next you will need a suitable set of coil spring compressors. There are many types on the market, but the ones to avoid come as a set of three – these tend to slip off. There are fairly inexpensive versions available with two compressors, each with a significant claw-style casting, which grips the spring solidly and prevents slipping. The garage trade tends to use a purpose-built machine to make this job easier and avoid damaging the paint on the springs, but you need to be changing a lot of springs to make investment in one of these machines worthwhile.

Apply the pressure from the spring compressors evenly. This is not to say that you need only do one turn at a time: depending on the rate of the spring, you'll be able to judge how many turns on one side feels all right before you switch to the other side.

Picture of the strut and spring with spring compressors fitted.

This inexact instruction may appear unhelpful, but when you undertake the task, it will seem perfectly logical. What you especially want to avoid is excessive bowing of the spring, which happens when the load is too heavily biased to one compressor.

Eventually you will get to a point where the top spring plate is clearly loose – this is an indication that the top nut on the damper is now safe to undo. Nevertheless, it is worth pointing out here that if the nut is undone and there is significant preload still in the spring, serious injury could result.

Step 12: Undo the top mounting nut once the pressure is released

Once you have undone the top nut, you can remove the spring from the damper. It is most important to note (ideally not just in your mind) the order in which the parts come off the spring and damper assembly. There will usually be a top nut, a washer, a top mount assembly including a bearing, quite often a spacer of some sort, followed by the upper spring seat. If reassembly isn't correct, it is entirely possible to cause the strut to bind up on the top mount. There are instances where people have sought softer springs when in actual fact the springs weren't the problem, it was because the suspension wasn't working at all. Such is the cushioning effect of the tyre that complete binding of the suspension on a sports vehicle isn't always as obvious as you'd expect it to be.

Then reverse the load you put into the spring compressors, not forgetting to alternate as you undo them. Even if you are fitting a coil-over unit

Undo the damper top nut once the spring is compressed enough.

replacement and you don't need the spring compressors, always unload them and store them away neatly. There is a temptation in the excitement to leave the compressed spring lying around somewhere. Although it is unlikely there would be a problem, anything to do with cars is much less likely to result in injury when you adopt a thorough approach, which puts safety first. The energy in the spring is considerable, and generally at its most extreme with heavy luxury cars, with double wishbone suspension. These will often run fairly stiff springs to cope with the loss ratio, and lots of preload to hold up the body. Extra care must be taken in these situations.

Step 13: Old damper compared to the new B14

Now is a good time to look at the old unit and the new one side by side. The most apparent difference is the size of the piston rod on each unit – though in actual fact identifying them both as piston rods isn't strictly correct. The original damper is a twin-tube design, which has a piston attached to the end of the rod protruding from the assembly; it is approximately 20mm in size. The Bilstein B14 replacement units is an inverted mono-tube design, and the piston is fixed inside the damper – what we perceive as the piston rod, protruding from the damper, is actually a tube that slides over the piston. We know the MacPherson strut design puts high side loadings into the strut.

Old damper compared to the new Bilstein B14 unit.

Tighten the top nut to a specified torque.

The inverted mono-tube design reduces the stiction experienced by the strut. 'Stiction' is the static friction that needs to be overcome to enable relative motion of stationary objects in contact. The term is a portmanteau of the words 'static' and 'friction'. The high side loadings on the strut under braking and acceleration affect its ability to move slowly in and out with the surface of the road.

By reducing the side loading, the damper is better able to work in harmony with the spring, to keep the tyre keyed into the road or track surface.

Step 14: Reassembling the top mount on the new B14
In most instances the next step is to install the original equipment top mount on to the new strut assembly. A lot of aftermarket kits are supplied with a new top mount, but it is worth remembering that these are often designed for track performance, and may well result in additional noise, vibration and harshness on a road vehicle.

Once the strut is back together, reassembly is the reversal of removal. This is easily said, but hard to do, and in reality the best thing you can do is check, and check again.

Step 15: Fit a new wishbone (and hub and driveshaft if changing)
Replace the hub and driveshaft if these have been removed, then install the new wishbone and connect the ball joint into the hub.

In this particular installation the wishbone being installed is wider than the one being removed, which has the effect of increasing the track width. The idea behind this is that in a front-wheel-drive vehicle with a lot of weight on the front wheels, it is most likely the front tyres are the ones that get overheated. Increasing the track width reduces the weight trans-

New wishbone installed.

fer on this axle, which means that cornering forces are more evenly applied by making the rear of the car transfer more of the load.

Step 16: Install the strut and spring assembly

If using a coilover assembly such as the Bilstein B14, you need to set the preload on the spring. The manufacturer may provide you with an optimal setting, in which case use this. However, some manufacturers may give you little or no information, in which case a good starting point must be selected, then work from there. What is most crucial is that you don't end up too low.

There are a number of different designs on the market. The Fiat design uses a bolted strut, which is easy to work with and also permits very easy adjustment of camber. The plug-type mounts are the opposite – they are not easy to work with, and

do not permit adjustment of camber at all, without machining work. If you need large amounts of negative camber on the bolted strut design, you can elongate the damper mounting holes, and either use a camber bolt with an eccentric adjustment, or simply position the strut manually to the desired camber position (the bolt holes on the strut would need elongating) and do the nuts up tight with quality high tensile bolts (usually 10.8 marking). Although it might seem as if movement would occur, in practice it doesn't.

Equally with the plug-type mounts you might sometimes wonder how you wouldn't lose steering control, as some designs do not have a location spigot. For a bolted type strut a camber bolt is generally the more reliable solution; alternatively for heavy duty use the damper bracket could be plated and redrilled, giving a solid mounting and fixed point. Of course before modifying a damper casing, oil and gas would need to be removed.

Install the strut.

Step 17: Tighten the top nut

Refit and tighten the damper to hub mounting bolts. Fit the top mount on to the chassis, and tighten the top nut. The torque on this piece is crucial: too much and it is extremely easy to snap off the top of the damper, making the car dangerous in a flash.

Tighten the top nut to the specified torque.

Step 18: Refit the drop link

Refit the anti-roll bar drop link to the strut. Some links pick up on to the wishbone, but it is most usual to see them attached to the damper in a MacPherson strut assembly. Check the assembly to make sure you haven't missed anything, then the front end can be lowered. The only thing left to do would be to adjust the toe and camber settings, but that can wait until the rear end is finished.

Refit the drop link to the strut.

Raise the rear of the car and support it on axle stands.

Step 19: Start the rear end

The front end of the car should now be finished. Make sure the wheels are done up to the correct torque, and now turn your attention to the back of the car. Firstly crack the initial torque off the rear wheel bolts, then safely raise the rear of the car and support it on stands.

Looking at the Panda 100HP, the rear suspension of the 169 version consists of a semi-independent beam axle. This is in contrast to the dead beam axle of its predecessor. The semi-independent beam axle suspension is extremely easy to work on. Changing out the springs and shocks on this type of arrangement is so straightforward: no spring compressors are required, and utilizing a jack ensures that it is easy to get the lower shock bolt in.

The rear assembly consists of a separate spring and damper. In common with a large number of vehicles, the spring and damper on the rear are not actually coilovers, a term that has really come to mean adjustable ride height, rather than strictly a coil-over-damper.

Step 20: Support the axle beam and remove the rear dampers

After supporting the axle beam using an appropriate jack, undo the top and bottom damper mounting bolts. Ensure that the ABS sensor and brake wear pad

Support the beam axle with a jack before undoing the damper mounting bolts.

wires, if fitted, are unclipped, because if they become overstretched they will break and need replacement.

Remove the dampers from both sides, ensuring there is no load so as to permit easy removal of the bolts – you don't want to undo the bolts without supporting the beam, as they will be very hard to remove and may actually get damaged in the process. Not to mention the danger of the beam suddenly dropping.

Step 21 – Lower the beam on the jack to permit spring removal

It is useful to have two jacks to carry out this operation – the factory scissor jack makes a useful beam support, while using your hydraulic jack to raise and lower the other side. Alternatively one jack and some wooden blocks will also work. Once you have removed the dampers you will be able to lower the beam down progressively, then remove the coil

With the shock removed, slowly lower the beam to remove the spring.

springs. Depending on the manufacturer's design and the type of spring fitted, you may need to push the beam down to be able to remove the spring. On some designs the spring may well have fallen out already.

Step 22: Install the adjustable spring mounts

The Bilstein design comes with an adjustable spring perch that enables you to add preload. In addition it also comes with its own bump stop, so it is necessary to remove the factory one.

If you do not, you will be riding on the factory bump stop too much, and the rear rate will be too high, causing instability. That said, it is possible to tune the handling and even to supplement the rate of the spring, using carefully chosen expanding foam bump stops. In order to do this you need access to force deflection curves to decide what works for you. If the kit you are fitting relies on the factory bump stop, then ensure it is in good condition. Very often manufacturers use the bump stop as a key component in the handling set-up, but if it isn't serviceable, then replace it.

Install the adjustable spring platform.

Remove the factory bump stop.

Step 23: Install the new springs and then the dampers

Replace both springs (if you do one side and fit the damper, you will then not be able to install the spring on the other side) and then fit the dampers. Remember to use the jack to ensure the bolt holes are correctly aligned. The bolt should thread by hand. If it does not, try realigning the bolt hole.

You should now have both shocks and springs installed.

Once the dampers are fitted it is generally good practice to leave final tightening until the vehicle is lowered. However, this isn't always the case, so check the vehicle-specific notes in an appropriate workshop manual. Refit the road wheels, and lightly seat the nuts/bolts.

Step 24: Finalizing the rear

Slowly and carefully lower the car off the stands, and ensure the wheels are torqued to the correct setting. Now is a good time to go back mentally and visually through the process, and make sure there is nothing

Comparison of the Original Damper and the Shorter Bilstein Unit

It is useful at this stage to compare the old and new rear dampers. You can see that the replacement unit is significantly shorter. This is because the replacement spring is significantly stiffer, which also means it is shorter. In order to ensure the spring is properly located in the axle beam, the damper must be shorter. This has the secondary effect of reducing droop, which ultimately limits roll.

Comparison of the original damper and the shorter Bilstein unit.

Install new springs and damper.

New rear shock and spring installed.

Fiat Panda 100HP with modified suspension through Paddock Bend at Brands Hatch, Kent.

Bilstein sticker in place.

that is left loose or perhaps without a fastening. If you have worked to a set of instructions, then the ride height is probably acceptable at this point.

Next, the car is best driven gently to ensure that no knocks or clonks occur. Initially the suspension could take a little while to settle, so arguably you could put a handful of miles on the vehicle. Oddly this is one occasion when speed humps are quite useful.

Step 25: Ride height optimization
If the kit came with a recommended height setting, this is usually best followed, as one would hope it was based on some science and testing. If not, the best approach is to ensure some rake from front to rear – that is, the front should be slightly lower than the rear. Too low can cause issues with roll centres. The lightest end of the car should have the lowest roll centre. It is easy to see how this common mistake

can be made on a FWD hatchback with MacPherson strut front suspension. In addition, the lowest end of the car should have the lowest roll centre – this is how a lot of people don't notice the fact that the lower roll centre on the front is causing so many issues, as it is on the lowest end of the car.

Step 26: Sticker and test drive
The real test, of course, is the first test drive to see if you have put everything back together properly.

The Panda 100HP attended a track day at Brands Hatch driven by three different drivers on the day: it provided excellent low cost thrills, and punched well above the lowly power-to-weight ratio that categorized it. Far from being a moving road block, at times it was seen with significantly quicker cars behind it and not catching it, lap after lap. Such is the importance of good corner speed to overall lap time.

CHAPTER FOUR

MODIFYING A SUSPENSION SYSTEM

Before embarking on any mission to modify a suspension system, it is vital to consider the objectives of the project. The almost ubiquitous coil spring and damper set-up is fraught with compromise. Even active suspension systems have some limiting factors.

It is abundantly clear that to take a dedicated 4WD off-road capable vehicle and try to turn it into an endurance racing prototype would be a foolish endeavour. A vehicle that is designed to take off-road loads is built in a very different way to a sealed tarmac race car.

However, this does not mean that there isn't a crossover. Take, for example, the Ariel Nomad, which is based on the Atom. You could easily take a small light hatchback and turn it into a bonafide circuit giant killer. You can make a good rally car from a hatchback. However, if you are driving through four feet of water and climbing steep inclines, then vehicles that are purpose-built for this tend to be big and heavy. Likewise, why make your life difficult getting a FWD hatch to win outright when you could use a mid-mounted rear-wheel-drive coupé instead.

The point here is that you need to select your starting material carefully. Buy the car that gives you the best chance to enjoy the road or track that you want to drive on. Should your goal be competitive motor sport, then study the regulations carefully, as you'll know what modifications can be made. It is senseless to buy three-way dampers with remote canisters and add them to a relatively standard vehicle, which then pushes you into a class featuring unlimited machinery.

So once the ideal vehicle is acquired, you can then start to write down the objective of the suspension tuning. For example, if a single-seater sprint or hillclimb racing car is being campaigned, the suspension will have to be carefully designed to work with optimized aerodynamics. The aim will be to break a known time, and to do that data and telemetry will drive the development of the suspension design. If it is a rallycross car, the objective will be a suspension system that gives a perfect blend of performance on the mixed surfaces.

Suspension is all about optimizing the tyres' contact with the surface. Coil springs and dampers are what the majority of people will be working with. However, many different systems have been built over the years, and it pays dividends to understand the strengths and weaknesses of the different layouts.

DIFFERENT SUSPENSION LAYOUTS

So if you wish to modify a suspension system, do you start with the best available layout, or build a new one?

Before starting to modify a suspension system it is worth considering the different suspension layouts and their foibles and virtues. Although there are still formulae today that use antiquated designs (such as Formula V, which stipulates the use of the original VW trailing arm design where roll angle = camber angle), it is best to start your quest by having the best set-up in the class. For example, if you decided to embark on a campaign in saloon racing you would find many options open to you. If you compare on paper an Alfa Romeo 156 with a VW Golf Mk4, you will see that the Alfa Romeo has a hugely superior suspension design. Does this mean you'll see more Alfa 156 race cars than Golf Mk4s? Possibly not. Other entrenched perceptions often see to it that inferior designs are still popular.

The logic is clear, though: always start with the best platform you can. The following pages describe the different suspension layouts so you can then work out if your chosen development car is going to be advantageous.

MACPHERSON STRUT

The MacPherson strut is a beautifully simple solution where the upper suspension arm is effectively located to the top mount. Dispensing with the upper arm brings cost savings, although the height of the suspension means it is rarely suited to single-seater or sports prototype cars. A further challenge of the MacPherson strut is the camber control, which can only be properly controlled through a fairly small range of motion. High corner loads will see the MacPherson strut add positive camber, just when it is least required.

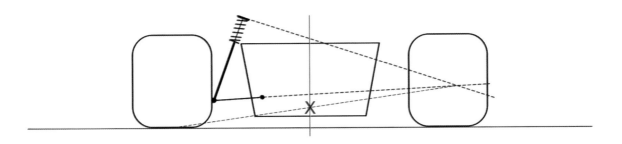

X = ROLL CENTRE

MacPherson strut suspension.

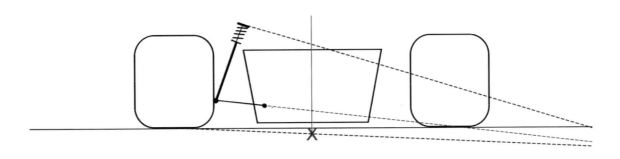

X = ROLL CENTRE

MacPherson strut suspension lowered too much.

Another issue is that without the upper arm, the damper is required to resist both accelerative and braking loads, this creates high side loadings and stiction. Although the roll centre is relatively well located, this can easily be spoiled by lowering the vehicle too far, which can drop the roll centre below ground. This then causes more weight transfer about the springs, and creates a dynamic roll centre that moves well outside the vehicle. Pushed to the limit MacPherson strut suspension in this situation will tend to experience a sudden weight transfer to the already heavily loaded outside front wheel.

It is starting to sound as if this isn't a suspension layout you'd really want. Consider, though, that Porsche have used MacPherson strut suspension on the front of the 911 for a long time, and that the latest GT 3RS version lapped the Nürburgring in under 7min. What this demonstrates is that once the engineers work *with* the weaknesses, rather than fight against them, the MacPherson strut is no handicap to outright performance.

MacPherson strut suspension is generally found on the front axle, though it is also used on the driven axle (first by Lotus, hence sometimes still referred to as the 'Chapman' strut). Notable examples include the 4WD Lancia Delta Integrale, the Subaru Impreza and the Mitsubishi Lancer EVO.

Modern versions of MacPherson exist, which seek to isolate the suspension from the steering inputs. Ford, and soon after Renault, were pioneers in this area. By allowing the hub to turn without turning the strut, torque steer is dramatically reduced. Toyota featured a system called 'Super Strut', which was much earlier on the Celica. This also isolated the steering axis from the top mount. However, like many seemingly 'new' developments, there is a suspension design that has kept the steering axis isolated from the suspension for much longer.

DOUBLE WISHBONE SUSPENSION

A double wishbone (or double A-arm) suspension layout adds an upper control arm, which isolates the suspension from the steering input. However, simply having double wishbone suspension is no guarantee of great performance. It is a very flexible system, which has had a myriad of different interpretations over the years, all with their own set of positives and negatives.

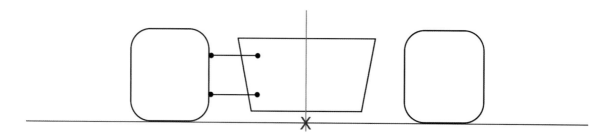

X = ROLL CENTRE

Double wishbone with arms of equal length and parallel.

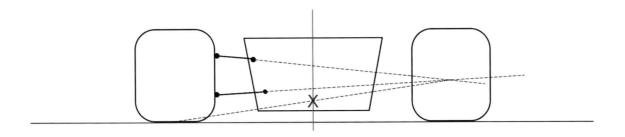

X = ROLL CENTRE

Double wishbone with arms of unequal length and non-parallel.

A double wishbone layout where the arms are of equal length and parallel might look elegant, but roll angle will lead to the same change in wheel angle in positive camber, and this is not good for a performance car. However, a double wishbone with arms of unequal length, not parallel, and of converging angles, gives the designer the most flexibility. Within a defined range of motion, careful design can make this set-up tick nearly all the boxes. Naturally it is just as much at home on the front or the rear axle.

Nowadays most modern Formula cars use a pushrod-type suspension with long control arms to give the desired control over the wheel, without the downsides of the conventional spring mounting on a double wishbone set-up.

LIVE AXLE AND DE DION

The live axle is an extremely simple design, and was once the norm on production cars. Encased in the live axle is the differential, and the drive shafts (known as half shafts).

The biggest downside of the live axle is the unsprung weight. Furthermore, in its simplest form, without multiple additional locating arms, it tends to have poor wheel control. However, with the use of fore and aft links, and a Panhard rod (or a watts

linkage), it is possible to locate a live axle so the wheel control is good. A good feature of a live axle is that there is no camber change through vertical movement. Space-frame oval Hot Rod racing cars are a good example of extremely fast machinery that uses this antiquated design. You could take a typical 1,600kg 500bhp production car on road tyres, and the chances are you wouldn't get close to a 250bhp Hot Rod on a typically short UK circuit.

Lydden Hill Circuit has sometimes seen a mixture of oval and MSA formula on the same day. It is good fun to watch, and no doubt some might pour scorn on the more budget oval formula, but when you see a Hot Rod run with the fastest class of MSA cars it is quite eye opening. They possess phenomenal cornering ability and are very adjustable on the limit. Strong under braking, the only weakness is a lack of bhp for the long straights. However, the power-to-weight ratio is good, and that helps everywhere else.

The De Dion has a similar roll-centre location to the live axle (mostly in the centre of the differential housing). However, where it scores over the live axle is that the heavy differential housing and drive flanges are bolted to the vehicle. This reduces the unsprung weight. The wheels are connected on either side by a tube, and then using either a coil or a leaf spring the

Alfa Romeo GTV6 with De Dion rear suspension featuring a Watts linkage.

wheel is only permitted to move vertically either by a sliding pillar-type arrangement, or multiple links. The advantage of a transverse leaf spring in this situation is that it can double as a top link connection.

Alfa Romeo is probably the most famous adopter of this technology, using it on the Alfa Romeo Alfetta, the GT, GTV, GTV6, Giulietta, Alfa 6, 90, 75/Milano, and the SZ/RZ. After many years of FWD vehicles, Alfa Romeo has produced the new RWD Giulia with a more modern multilink rear suspension.

THE BEAM AXLE

A beam axle is the 'dead' version of a live axle. Solidly connecting both wheels together, the beam axle is the norm in light and medium trucks, and also very popular on vehicles with off-road capability. It has the same disadvantages as the live axle, namely high unsprung weight, no opportunity to design favourable

camber change, and chiefly the lack of independent control. However, its beauty is in its simplicity, and it is also tough and durable – for example, compare the number of bushings on an independent wishbone suspension to a simple beam axle.

By virtue of excellent articulation over uneven surfaces this arrangement is still extremely popular. However, it is not something you are likely to see on many racing circuits, unless they involve extreme off-road competition.

TORSION BEAM AXLE

Torsion beam axle is arguably still the most popular rear suspension layout on compact front-wheel-drive cars. Although at first sight it may appear not to be independent, a surprising amount of uncon-nected wheel movement is obtained with this type of suspension. It is therefore generally known as

The Panhard Rod

The Panhard rod is one of the simplest and most time-honoured methods in suspension design. It was invented by Panhard et Levassor of the Panhard motor company, and was used on their cars in the early 1900s.

Optimal suspension design seeks to control the wheel so that its movement is only vertical. Lateral and longitudinal movement is undesirable. A Panhard rod is designed to control lateral movement of an axle. The rod is located in two positions, one on the bodyshell, and the other on the suspension beam (or arm). By using a bushing at each mount, the rod permits vertical movement, but it effectively stops lateral movement by being in tension or compression, depending on which way the car is rounding the corner.

The Panhard rod is generally seen on off-road and 4x4 vehicles, but it is also seen in high-performance RWD applications where a live axle is still used. Here a Panhard rod is often fitted in conjunction with fore and aft links that prevent longitudinal movement.

Some small front-wheel-drive cars have also employed a Panhard rod to increase the prowess of their rear suspension, notably the Nissan Micra and Toyota Starlet.

The one major downside to the Panhard rod is that it forces the axle to move in an arc, the shape of which is defined by the length of the rod. This is why you will see that most Panhard rods are nearly as long as the axle beam themselves, to reduce the effect of this movement.

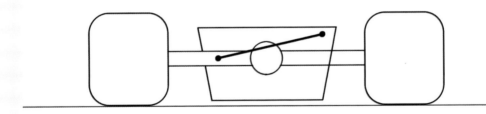

Panhard rod.

The Watts Linkage

The Watts linkage was invented by James Watt and described in the patent for his 1784 steam engine. It is like a Panhard rod that is split in the middle, with a third connecting link. The two long links are of equal length, while the third interconnecting link is shorter. The Watts linkage fundamentally solves the weakness of the Panhard rod. It prevents lateral movement of the axle, but during the majority of the range of motion the central link moves only in a vertical motion, with no sideways movement.

At the extremes of movement the central point of the short linkage deviates from a straight line. The shape that is formed by this trace is a figure-of-eight. This is known as 'Watts curve'. There is an excellent animation of this linkage in motion at this URL https://upload.wikimedia.org/wikipedia/commons/9/93/Watts_linkage.gif

Some stills from the animation show that at extremes of movement, deviation from the centre point is noted.

Although not conveying truly straight motion about a centre point at extremes of movement, the vehicle designer can make the Watts linkage operate within the stroke of the suspension in such a way. This can be achieved by limiting droop travel and ensuring that compressive travel occurs in the correct range for the Watts linkage.

Although this is an old piece of technology it was recently used in an innovative way by Vauxhall/Opel on the Astra rear suspension. On the higher performance derivatives the semi-independent beam axle was supplemented by a Watts linkage to ensure better wheel control. The Watts linkage enabled a more compliant bushing on the beam body mount to reduce noise, whilst still offering improved wheel control. Unfortunately this fitment isn't appearing on newer Astra models, so thanks to Sea Place Garage in Worthing, a photograph of the linkage was taken.

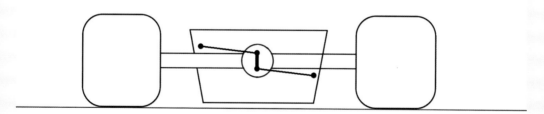

Watts linkage.

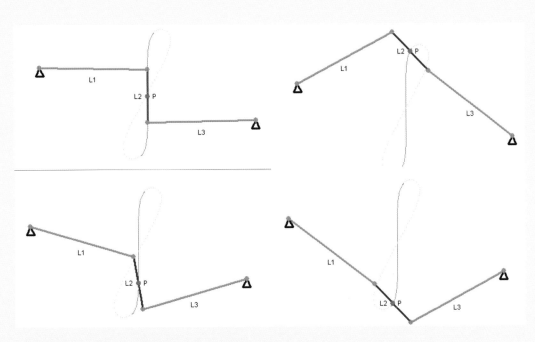

Stills from an online animation of a Watts linkage.

Vauxhall Astra with Watts linkage to improve the kinematics of the semi-independent beam axle suspension.

semi-independent suspension. The torsion beam axle is designed to offer a degree of camber and toe change depending on the mounting orientation. However, the geometry change is relative to the difference in position between the left and right wheels. For example, as the vehicle rolls and the axle is twisted, the outer wheel is pushed up, and the inner wheel, being unloaded by the weight transfer, will push down. In this situation there is camber gain on the outside wheel.

If both wheels rise and fall at the same time – for example, when traversing a speed bump in the road – then there isn't any camber or toe change, and the system behaves much like a beam axle.

Due to the semi-independent nature of the suspension, there is also a degree of coupling between the left and right wheel. This creates an anti-roll effect, and is dependent on the stiffness of the beam. Some vehicles are able to dispense with the rear anti-roll bar, notably the Fiat Punto Mk2 in 1999, a car that didn't suffer from excess understeer, but also didn't need a rear anti-roll bar. The downside, though, is that reducing the semi-independent nature of the suspension can provoke more of a reaction over single-wheel bumps. Most examples nowadays tend to feature fairly ductile axle beams, and then a variety of anti-roll bars are fitted depending on the intended specification of the vehicle. For example, an L-specification vehicle will feature a smaller anti-roll bar than the R specification of the same car.

The torsion-beam axle system is simple, reasonably light, and cheap to manufacture; it doesn't intrude into the vehicle's interior space, and is still used by a number of makers for these reasons.

Of course, because it isn't the most sophisticated system, and does have a number of downsides, it is often scoffed at. However, where used on the rear of the front-wheel-drive car, it is not the handicap that many would have you believe.

INDEPENDENT TRAILING ARM

The independent trailing arm type of suspension often tends to have an axle beam, however this tends to be mounted to the body by rubber bushings, and doesn't move much. Movement in the suspension occurs by virtue of the trailing arms, which are allowed to pivot in the axle tube independently from each other. This is usually facilitated by the use of bearings and a stub axle.

The method of springing is also variable, and it could be torsion bars, or coil springs. For example, the Peugeot 205 used torsion bars, and the Fiat Coupé used coil springs.

The biggest benefit in this set-up is the independent nature of the suspension. The biggest downside is that the camber angle will equal roll angle, so 3 degrees of roll is 3 degrees of positive camber. On the front axle this would be extremely difficult to manage, although in the case of a front-wheel-drive vehicle, this characteristic is not as bad as it sounds, since a front-wheel-drive car is very much driven on the front wheels, and ideally the rear is a compliant partner in the affair. It is telling that both the FWD Peugeot 205 and Fiat Coupé have set scintillating lap times around tracks when properly prepared.

In fact Peugeot engineered in passive rear steer effects to the 205 (and indeed to the 106, 309 and 306) to make it feel more responsive to steering input, while BMW did the same thing on the new Mini. From a sealed tarmac racing perspective, these passive rear steer characteristics actually start to become unhelpful. Therefore it is usually best to replace the flexible rubber bushings with stiffer polyurethane, and even nylon or aluminium. Fitted to the standard vehicle, this type of bushing would just create more noise, and possibly dull the handling responses. Used together with extremely stiff springs and much bigger anti-roll bars, it allows the engineer to dial in the required handling response, without an unmanaged passive component interfering.

SWING AXLE

The swing has achieved a degree of notoriety, and you won't have to speak to too many people who understand car suspension, to be told a story about a near miss, or a crash, or worse, as a result of this type of suspension.

The benefit over a live axle or beam axle is reduced unsprung weight – when driven, the differential will usually be mounted to the body. When

Jacking Forces

Jacking forces are the total of the vertical force experienced by the suspension links.

With a roll centre above ground the jacking forces are upward; if the roll centre is below ground, then the jacking forces are downward.

Some suspension designs have a roll centre that is a long way above ground level, and these can cause fairly extreme jacking forces, as the effect of lifting the body up above the suspension creates droop in the suspension. If the camber (and toe) curve of the suspension is unfavourable, then this jacking force will generally lose grip and make the vehicle unstable.

A good example of this is the swing-axle style of suspension. The high roll centre creates an increasing vertical jacking force under lateral cornering loads. Interestingly, within Formula One aerodynamic advantages have been achieved by using a downward jacking force. This requires a roll centre below ground level, which is generally considered to be undesirable; however, it must be considered with regard to the very limited suspension movement in a modern Formula One car.

The front-wheel-drive Fiat 128 and Strada (Ritmo) featured this arrangement on the rear, and it certainly makes for exciting handling on the limit. However, it is nothing like the widow-maker tendencies of the same arrangement with a driven rear axle such as the Triumph Spitfire or Chevrolet Corvair. The actor James Dean died in the swing axle-equipped Porsche 550 Spyder. For many years Dean was seen as a rebel who drove excessively fast – probably millions of T shirts have been sold with the printed adage 'Too fast to live, too young to die'.

Detailed investigation of the crash shows that Dean actually braked very hard, rather than accelerated around the other car involved in the accident. The heavy braking would have caused a significant front weight transfer, unloading the rear wheels, which would then move into droop and gain positive camber. At this point the steering inputs applied would make the vehicle unstable. So it's certainly possible that had Dean been driving a front-engined Ferrari with a live axle, and not a mid-engined Porsche with a swing axle, he might have survived that day.

In short, if it's got a swing axle, try to keep the speeds a little lower if you want to get home

James Dean and Porsche speedster #23F at Palm Springs Races, March 1955.

you first look at the camber curve on compression there is favourable negative camber change, however there is potentially destabilizing positive camber change during extension. In addition, although negative camber can be created through roll, it is possible for the tyre to gain more grip, suddenly, at a transient point in the corner. This can cause the chassis to jack upwards, and then the outside wheel starts to generate positive camber. It can also cause a fishtailing effect as the driver attempts to correct each movement – the reaction seems to be stronger than the action, and the inevitable loss of control follows shortly after. In extreme cases it can overturn the vehicle. The jacking forces are very high as a result of the high roll centre.

SLIDING PILLAR AND SLIDING AXLE

This suspension first appeared on the French Decauville of 1898. This type of suspension is somewhat bizarrely still in use today on Morgans – although it is argued by many that the Morgan version should be referred to as 'sliding axle' and not as 'sliding pillar'. Another description is 'inverted sliding pillar'. Regardless of the semantics, the two designs are similar, and in practice they both work in the same way, in that the wheel is permitted vertical movement between two fixed points by the use of springs and guide bearings.

Morgan actually patented their system in 1910, but there is very little chance of any car manufacturer seeking to license this system. Indeed, arguably, due to the similarity of preceding designs, the patent would never have stood up to scrutiny. The biggest downside of the system is that the track width varies as the suspension moves up and down. However, it does still offer good control of camber, which is more important. So perhaps that is why this anachronism exists to this day.

PUSH-ROD AND PULL-ROD SUSPENSION

The majority of formula racing cars now use some version of push-rod or pull-rod suspension. Both suspension systems enable the damper and spring to be

Sliding pillar suspension on the front of a 1938 Alta racing car at Brooklands Museum, Weybridge.

Morgan's inverted sliding pillar/sliding axle.

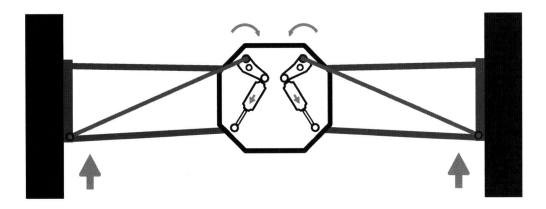

Diagram showing a pushrod suspension system.

mounted inboard, bringing a reduction in unsprung weight and significant aerodynamic benefits. Both operate in a similar fashion – the pull-rod design is essentially an inverse of the push-rod, so the units will be mounted much lower. Most F1 cars use push-rod designs due to aerodynamic restraints that make the pull-rod harder to implement.

A significant advantage of push-rod suspension over conventional double wishbone is the ability, using the leverage of the rocker arm, to return the suspension motion ratio closer to, or at 1:1. The motion ratio with conventional double wishbone requires larger, heavier springs to give the same wheel rate as a suspension without a motion ratio.

Until fairly recently Caterham also used a push-rod system on the CSR models, but sadly this has now been scrapped and all current Caterhams use a conventional double wishbone. Just as Citroën have scrapped the hydro-pneumatic, it is sometimes the case that even when a system proves to be better, it may not be commercially successful.

The next things to consider are spring rates, suspension frequency, and pitch optimization.

SPRING RATES

After choosing your preferred layout, or simply realizing more about the suspension a vehicle is equipped with, it is crucial to look at spring rate and how this interacts with the tyre and the vehicle body. The requirements will depend on use – for example racing stiff, minimal travel; forest rally soft, long travel – so as well as the rate used, you also have to consider the amount of movement. The primary objective when choosing springs, from the perspective of both chassis and engine, is to prevent them going coil bound. This is not the same as when a progressive suspension spring brings one or more coils together, and consequently increases the spring rate. Coil bound is when all the coils are touching, and there is no more give in the spring: it is acting as if it were solid.

If a spring goes coil bound on a race car it will result in a sudden weight transfer to that wheel, and this will usually overcome the grip of the tyre and result in a spin. If the spring goes coil bound on a rally car it is much more likely to happen after going airborne, and the resultant increase in rate will probably result in a broken suspension component and possibly a serious accident.

Knowing the amount of travel required is really based on the conditions. If the car is staying in touch with the ground, then the fastest suspension systems on tarmac with a slick tyre will tend to have very little movement. Conversely a forest rally system may see a car going airborne for quite some way, and it will therefore take some judgement to account for the kinetic energy and the amount of travel that the suspension will need. In fact in the field of rally suspension one tends to see some of the highest prices, because the rigour of the events requires a sufficiently sophisticated damper.

Coil springs are available in a wide range of sizes. The factors involved in the calculation of the spring are the wire diameter, the inside diameter and the number of active coils. It is possible with a formula to make a fairly good attempt at calculating the actual rate of a spring you have in hand. The formula is:

$$\text{spring rate} = GD4/8ND3$$

where:

G = torsional modulus steel
D = wire diameter in inches
N = number of active coils
D = mean coil diameter in inches. Mean diameter is (ID+OD)/2

If you worked it with a wire diameter of ½in (12.7mm) and a spring ID of 3in (76.2mm) with eight active coils (the whole working coil), the rate would be 325lb/in (6.25kg/Fmm). Changing the spring ID to 5in (the kind of size you see on a production vehicle) makes the rate only 77lb/in (1.38kg/Fmm). So often what you see on a typical modern saloon car with a MacPherson strut, is fewer coils to get the rate back. If the coils come down to four the rate moves to 154lb/in (2.75kg/Fmm).

Although this calculation is fairly accurate, testing is the best way to establish the rate of the spring. However, this method is particularly useful when you are told that the spring rate is 'not available' due to it being top secret. Usually most of the spring makers publish the spring wire diameter, the OD and number of working coils even when the rate itself is not revealed.

WHEEL RATE

You will hear spring rates being bandied around, and sometimes this might be helpful, but at other times it may confuse or be incorrect. What is really important is the wheel rate. Different spring rates are really only comparable if they are used on a suspension of similar design. So for example a MacPherson strut suspension has a design where the spring centreline is very close to the ball-joint pivot point. This makes the wheel rate and spring rate very similar, with minimal loss. On the other hand a double wishbone suspension will often have a substantial difference between the spring centreline and the ball-joint pivot point. This creates a loss ratio, meaning that the wheel rate will be less than the spring rate.

The formula in this instance is:

$$MR = D1/D2$$

So take the S-type Jaguar front suspension as a good example of the double wishbone (perhaps more accurately called a high upper wishbone, lower L-arm suspension).

Here is an easy way to visualize the D1/D2 calculation. In this instance figures achieved on the Jaguar S-type were 240mm for D1 and 360mm for D2, giving a motion ratio of 0.67.

What does the motion ratio allow us to work out? Simply with the formula below you can work out the wheel rate from the spring rate. The formula is:

$$\text{wheel rate} = \text{spring rate} \times (\text{motion ratio}^2)$$

In the instance of the Jaguar S-type, the spring measurements were difficult to gauge with the lack of a spring rate tester, as the spring changed in ID from large at the top mounting, to narrow at the bottom spring plate. So an estimation of rate based on average diameter was made, where the front spring rate is approximately 300lb/in.

Jaguar S-type front suspension motion ratio calculation.

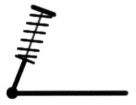

ANGLE OF SPRING CAUSES FALLING RATE ON DEFLECTION

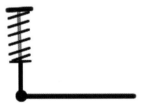

SPRING AT 90 DEG RATE REMAINS CONSTANT ON DEFLECTION

Spring angle deflection.

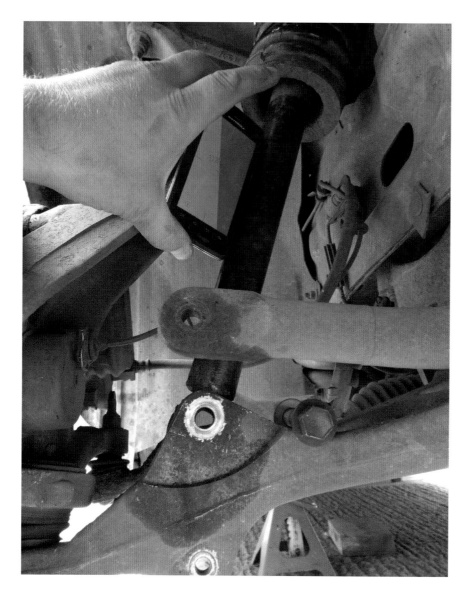

Jaguar S-type front spring angle measurement.

So with the ratio of 0.67 squared being 0.4489, the wheel rate is approximately 134lb/in. In terms of spring frequency this is very soft suspension, in keeping with the Jaguar ethos of a smooth ride. It does make up for this lack of spring rate in roll with the large 32mm hollow front anti-roll bar. Being hollow it will be difficult to work out the stiffness of this bar without knowing the wall thickness, but there is no doubt that Jaguar have used the anti-roll bars to control the roll rather than the springs.

However, the formula given simplifies things somewhat, and is really only acceptable to use where the spring is close to vertical. As you can see from the image below, as the angle of the spring changes, the wheel rate is reduced as deflection increases. This amount is fairly negligible at small angles, but increasingly important as the angles move beyond 20 degrees.

A better formula, then, to cater for the angle correction is:

wheel rate = spring rate x (motion ratio^2) x spring angle correction

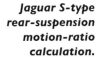

Jaguar S-type rear-suspension motion-ratio calculation.

To obtain the spring angle correction (SAC) you need to calculate

SAC = (Cosine A) x C

The spring angle on the Jaguar could be found by 3D modelling, but with the widespread use of mobile phones and applications, measurement is fairly easy, even with a classic like the Droid 4 from Motorola.

The spring angle on the Jaguar was 18 degrees. Cosine (COS) of 18 degrees is 0.95, so the actual wheel rate on the Jaguar S-type was (134) x (0.95) = 127lb/in (2.27kg/Fmm).

On the rear of the S-type the motion ratio was 0.6214: squared this becomes 0.386, which is a greater loss ratio than the front. The spring measurements are approximate as the outer diameter changes slightly, but working on a median the rear spring rate is approximately (again for accurate spring rates a spring must be tested) 500lb/in (8.93kg/Fmm). The wheel rate then is approximately 193lb/in (3.45kg/Fmm). Taking into account the angle correction factor (12 degrees = .978), the wheel rate is 189lb/in (3.38kg/Fmm).

SUSPENSION FREQUENCY

Knowing the frequency of a vehicle suspension is the best way to understand its stiffness. The natural frequency of the suspension is the rate at which it will move up and down in cycles per second (hertz). In much the same way as a loudspeaker or induction system is tuned to take advantage of resonant frequencies, suspension frequency is used to optimize the vehicle for its purpose.

As we have seen, the wheel rate on a suspension system can be very different to the spring rate. When we are looking at suspension frequency, it is the sprung weight of the vehicle and the wheel rate that are at play. The best way to think about this is the influence of carrying passengers. As the vehicle weight increases, the suspension frequency reduces, effectively resulting in softer suspension. Conversely, as weight is removed from a vehicle, sprung weight is reduced, and the suspension frequency increases. In addition, in both cases the ride height will move. For example, preparing a car for competition use will see reductions in weight of 15 to 30 per cent as non-essential items are removed, which will leave the vehicle sat much higher than normal.

$$\text{frequency (hertz)} = 3.13 \sqrt{\frac{\text{wheel rate}}{\text{sprung weight}}}$$

Suspension frequency formula.

Calculating suspension frequency is relatively easy once we know the wheel rate and the sprung weight. The formula is shown in the picture below:

In order to calculate the sprung weight of each corner of the vehicle, firstly the vehicle must be weighed, and then account taken of the unsprung weight. Unsprung weight is the wheel and tyre and hub assembly, and most of the spring and damper. Part-unsprung weight includes items such as the wishbone, where only half of its weight is considered unsprung, along with other items where only a portion of the weight is unsprung, such as driveshafts, suspension links/control arms and dampers. Due to the structure of the formula that calculates suspension frequency, it is acceptable to make an estimate of unsprung weight.

At the very least, though, one would expect to weigh the wheel and tyre assembly and the hub/brake assembly. If you are just working out rough and ready figures without access to the vehicle, then something like 15kg for a lightweight sports car to 50kg for a larger saloon, wouldn't be far off.

Reducing unsprung weight is seen as a religion by many. Certainly the benefits are considerable, particularly for the wheel, which, due to being rotated, if lightened, actually has the same effect as more horsepower. Small bumps are better navigated by a light wheel, and the vehicle with low unsprung weight will have better grip over an imperfect surface. However, the downside is that it is less good at soaking up vibration, so when the road gets really bad, the irregularities of the surface will transfer through the suspension and into the body.

This is one of the reasons why SUV-style vehicles with big, heavy wheels and tyres have become popular – in essence it is partly due to the state of the roads! What they cannot mask, though, are the really big bumps where there is so much more energy in the moving mass of the wheel and tyre, which is why the control arms and subframe bushes have a lot of flex via rubber bushings to damp this noise.

Once we know the sprung weight, the unsprung weight and the wheel rate, the frequency is easy to calculate. The majority of vehicles will be in the range of 1 to 2 hertz. A luxury saloon will tend to have a low frequency, so that movements are relatively slow and predictable. 1 hertz would equate to a very leisurely walking pace, perhaps strolling around a museum – you would be unlikely to spill a drink at this pace. Conversely, walking briskly will see the pace closer to 2Hz, and at this speed you would not be able to hold a full drink without some spillage.

Walking is a useful analogy, because once the suspension frequency goes beyond 2Hz, most people would start to think it was firm, bordering on slightly uncomfortable.

Sports cars will tend to have a spring frequency around 2Hz, and this gives them a feeling of being responsive and stable. Higher frequencies are to be found in some more modern high performance cars, as the integrity of the chassis has allowed stiffer suspension to be used, without the kind of scuttle shake and shimmy that older, more flexible designs of the past offered.

The ideal suspension frequency can partly be defined by the use of the vehicle, in addition the choice of tyre and aerodynamics has a key impact. A slick racing tyre will generate far more lateral grip, at higher vertical loads than a road tyre. This necessitates the use of a higher suspension frequency, exact load data for the tyre would dictate this, but it is not uncommon to see more than 3Hz being used. This is all before aerodynamics gets involved, and makes things more difficult by increasing speed and adding even more vertical load.

We know from high-level single-seater motor sport that huge downforce can be generated, and the springs must take account of this. If the racing regulations are relatively free, then it may be possible to use a third spring. The third spring will not activate during roll, only during compressive loads applied equally to both wheels. This kind of design can permit the use of radical aerodynamics without resorting to the need for such excessively stiff wheel frequency that the vehicle becomes uncontrollable in certain conditions.

However, even in Formula One, the use of a third spring to take this aerodynamic load is not allowed. Many years ago the Chaparral racing car was to get banned by putting the aerodynamic load directly into the upright, therefore forcing the tyre into the ground without compressing the suspension. It does make you wonder just how fast modern Formula One cars would go if they were given a free rein in aerodynamics.

At the time of starting this book the original plan was to develop the seemingly overweight Jaguar S-type and modify it, hopefully to compete with factory-fresh sports coupés and hot hatches, for example the Renault Clio Sport, Porsche Boxster, Nissan 350Z. Comparisons would be based on track day and sprint performance against a range of vehicles. Clearly driver variance will somewhat cloud the results, but it will be easy to establish if clear improvements have been made. Unfortunately time and budget constraints prevented the project being finished, but some insights are gained through the reduction of weight, the analysis of the suspension and replacement of control arms.

Jaguar have always had a reputation for smooth-riding cars, and the S-type was no exception. The front spring gave a wheel rate of just 127lb/in. This might be sporty in a Caterham which weighs very little, but in the hefty 1,650kg Jaguar the frequency of the front suspension is just 1.21Hz, and the rear frequency 1.48Hz. Putting it very much in limousine territory, this is to be expected, of course, as a chassis designer should be designing the vehicle to suit its intended purpose.

So how did Jaguar resolve the sporting nature of the car with such soft springing? This was achieved via the anti-roll bar, which on the front axle is a mighty 32mm. This means that although the car rides in a very serene fashion, it still exhibits a front end with lots of grip and good roll control. This is partly a virtue of the short long arm (SLA) suspension (also sometimes called high double-wishbone). By having a shorter upper arm, negative camber is added through the compression stroke of the sus-

Walking Frequency

In a 2005 study the authors A. Pachi and Tianjian Ji investigated the stepping frequency and velocity of people walking. It considered 800 measurements on two footbridges and two shopping floors. During the measurements, the participants were not aware that they were being observed and walked naturally. The measurements of walking frequency, velocity and step length were processed using statistical methods, and the stepping frequency and velocity of the walking determined. It was found that (a) on shopping floors the people walked with an average frequency of 2.0Hz and a velocity of 1.4m/s, but on the footbridges they walked with an average frequency of 1.8Hz and a velocity of 1.3m/s; (b) the people's step length on the shopping floors and the footbridges was almost the same, with average values of 0.75m for men and 0.67m for women; (c) the men walked with a higher velocity than the women, while the women walked with higher frequency than the men; and (d) there was a linear relationship between walking velocity and frequency which was different for the men and the women.

pension. This is a more sophisticated design than the MacPherson strut, but it does have a downside, and that is the relatively high loss ratio, which means the spring has to be more than twice as stiff to get the chosen wheel rate.

One of the first things to assess is what spring rate will be needed to achieve a 2.0–2.5Hz suspension frequency. As we will soon discuss in the section on pitch optimization, the rear suspension frequency should ideally be stiffer than the front. The vehicle will need to be used on the road, and in wet and dry conditions. For simplicity there will be no extensive aerodynamic modifications, so frequency between two and two-and-a-half cycles a second should be a good starting point.

One way to increase the stiffness of the existing suspension is to remove weight. Losing weight in a car is a virtuous circle: you lose weight and the car accelerates faster, corners faster, there is less braking energy required and less tyre wear, the outright cornering speed increases – and so it goes on in a circle, where the reduction of weight has impact in multiple areas.

THE SIGNIFICANCE OF CHASSIS STIFFNESS

Chassis stiffness is close to godliness when considered with reference to its importance in the field of suspension. Unlike a kart, where some flex in the chassis is an integral part of the set-up, the saloon or single-seater racing car works best when the chassis is as rigid as possible. What might be surprising to the reader is to learn just how much movement can occur in what is seemingly a rigid structure. For example, if you were to weld a roll cage into an eighties hatchback, you would notice that if you pushed your finger into the gap between the cage tube and the windscreen surround, you would find as you reversed off a steeply inclined driveway on to the road, that at some point your finger will get slightly squashed. It obviously required an inquisitive mind to try this for the first time, and clearly one of your hands, which might be useful for steering, is out of action during this moment. But what it dem-

onstrates in a way that is always more powerful than the written word, is just how much a supposedly stiff chassis flexes.

CHASSIS STIFFNESS

Chassis stiffness is a crucial aspect of modern car design, and a vital tool in the armoury of the race tuner seeking to improve the dynamics of an existing vehicle. By making the chassis stiff, the loads that pass through it during cornering have less of an effect on its position.

Research has shown that car manufacturers are making stiff chassis to give a 'premium feel'. Quantifying if this makes any difference to performance is harder. Unwanted chassis flex could cause geometry problems and prevent a tyre from delivering its optimal vertical load performance. Again it is interesting to consider a kart, because with no suspension, theoretically a stiffer chassis is best. Unfortunately the ostensibly simple kart is just as technical to set up as a car, and experience shows that if the chassis is too stiff, the kart won't be quick. Of course, part of this is due to the locked rear axle.

One of the most popular modifications is a strut brace. This is a lateral brace connecting the strut towers together, or in the case of the double wishbone, each side of the top mounting. Many people will scoff at such a modification, and suggest that if it were necessary the manufacturer would have fitted it as standard. The reality is that many do when they launch a high-performance version of a standard model; for example the BMW M3 E46, the Lancia Delta Integrale and the Renault 19 16V all come with a strut brace on the front strut towers.

As with any modification to a vehicle, the best way to experience it is from the driving seat. The author has personally fitted a number of strut braces and has instantly been able to feel the benefit. This is where is gets complicated, because even if something feels better, this doesn't necessarily make the car faster. Nevertheless 'seat of the pants' feel generally bears out the engineering logic, because if you have two strut towers 1.5m apart and you add a brace between them, as long as the material specifications are up to scratch, you will be increasing lateral stiffness.

It is interesting to imagine a long, narrow canal boat at this point: if you have driven one, you'll know about the lag between steering input and reaction. This is to do with the length of the vessel and steering from the rear. It is also a good way to visualize the effect that tightening a chassis can give: it sharpens responses, reduces overhang of forces, and also enables the engineer to study the chassis more easily, as a stiff chassis throws up fewer variables.

One company, Koenigsegg, has made chassis stiffness integral to everything they do. The following is an excerpt from their website.

A Chevrolet Cruze is a generic, modern compact car. It has a torsional rigidity figure of 17,600Nm per degree.

The Mini Cooper from early this century is a more sporting economy car. It has a torsional rigidity figure of 24,500Nm per degree.

The Ferrari F50 is a performance car legend and a true collectible. It had a torsional rigidity figure of 34,600Nm per degree.

The Porsche 918 Spyder is a contemporary of the Agera, also with a removable roof. It has a torsional rigidity figure of 40,000Nm per degree.

The monocoque in the Koenigsegg Agera RS has a torsional rigidity figure of 65,000Nm per degree.

Chassis stiffness is therefore core to what this company does. A stiff chassis stops resonance, lets the suspension work without auxiliary factors, and generally contributes to the feeling of cohesiveness, as if the vehicle were hewn from granite.

One of the biggest changes in modern car design and production has been ever increasing chassis stiffness. Each successive generation of vehicle has sought to be stiffer than the last, so much so that a modern production hatchback could easily be as stiff as an older vehicle that had been comprehensively race prepared with a seam-welded shell and

Chaparral 2a racing car – stiff for its time, but flexible by modern standards.

a multipoint chromium molybdenum steel roll cage. This is genuinely startling when you think about it, and various television productions have shown just how outgunned an original hatchback is by its latest version (assuming power-to-weight ratios are vaguely similar).

What impact does this have if you are thinking of building a race car from a production car? Simply that a more modern design is very often hugely superior, even when a bit heavier. There was a time when the old 'classics' were faster than their more modern brethren. Think back to the Mk2 16-valve Golf versus the Mk3 2.0 16v. There was a moment when things were just getting heavier, but modern design has now shown, partly driven by safety regulations, that the incredibly stiff chassis permits exceptional cornering prowess.

So what is stiff and what is floppy? It is useful to look at the rates of other vehicles – the highs and lows – so you can make judgements on stiffness. For example, in 1963 Jim Hall and Hap Sharp built the Chaparral 2 racing car. At the time its chassis construction was considered radical – not dissimilar in construction to a modern Lotus Elise, it consisted of bonded box sections forming a monocoque. The design objective was to achieve 3,000lb-ft/degree (4,067Nm/degree). At the time it was considered the stiffest racing chassis.

It is useful to have the Chaparral as a yardstick for measurement, as a good example of a 'floppy' modern car is a BMW Z3 with 5,600Nm/deg of stiffness. This suddenly doesn't seem so bad, as it is 39 per cent stiffer than the Chaparral. However, by modern standards it is woeful.

Compare that to the BMW 5 Series (E39) with 24,000Nm/deg, and you can see the difference between an incredibly stiff saloon (even by today's standards) and a very flexible convertible. In fact it is interesting to note that during the contentious period where Rover was under BMW control, Rover were very keen to point out that their engineers had achieved 27 per cent more chassis stiffness with the MGF, and that this became even stiffer with the MG TF. In fact if you want to understand how chassis stiffness feels, you could try driving a Z3 Convertible and then jump into an MG TF: the TF will feel much stiffer right from the start, particularly if the roof is down in both cars.

Mazda, even on the NC version of the MX5 (Mk3), didn't better the MG TF. So what is at work here? How can an under-resourced Rover build a stiffer chassis than the mighty BMW? What is likely to have happened is that from the very start the Rover engineers set about building in stiffness, whereas the BMW may well have been created, and then assessed, and then found to be wanting. It is interesting how you see such divergence in these figures, almost as if some design teams thought that chassis stiffness was just not required.

But when you think about it, what is the point in making an ultra-stiff chassis if a vehicle is supposed to be driven at moderate speeds on the road? Arguably it's not really an issue if the spring frequency is low, and this could indeed explain some of the variances. So perhaps it makes more sense to look at this in reverse. In terms of chassis stiffness, if you want to run spring frequencies in the order of 1.5Hz then even 5,000Nm/deg isn't really enough. Ideally something like 10,000Nm/deg would be the minimum, and increasing as the frequency rose. 2.0Hz would probably be best with at least 15,000Nm/deg.

In fact a Society of Automotive Engineers (SAE) paper was published by L. Thompson, P. Soni, S. Raju and E. Law called 'The Effects of Chassis Flexibility on Roll Stiffness of a Winston Cup Race Car'. In it they tried to put a number on the minimum chassis stiffness required where you could say that it no longer had much effect on roll stiffness. Up to a point adding more chassis stiffness increases the roll stiffness by making the suspension more effective. They discovered that the minimum torsional stiffness required so that the effective roll stiffness of the front suspension was within 3 per cent from the roll stiffness with a rigid chassis, was about 23,100ft-lb/deg (31,319Nm/deg).

Even the mightily stiff E39 BMW 5 Series doesn't meet this figure. However, it would if it were stiffened and reinforced with a roll cage. Out of the box the Alfa Romeo 159 has a figure of 31,400Nm/deg, which puts it just above the figure referred to in the SAE paper.

These figures are hard to come by, but a McLaren F1 is alleged to have 13,500Nm/deg, which would make the Alfa Romeo 159 132 per cent stiffer than arguably the greatest super car of all time.

Is there any need for any more stiffness than this? If you are going to run very high spring frequency to counteract aerodynamic loads, then the chassis would ideally need something like 40,000Nm/deg. In this respect consider the Koenigsegg Agera R with 65,000Nm/deg and the Bugatti Veyron at 60,000Nm/deg.

As in any field of engineering, faced with restrictions and problems, clever solutions are often developed. Take a look at the Porsche 911 and try to construct a cogent argument that the engine is in the wrong place.

Alfa Romeo made a Targa Florio winning masterpiece of a car in the Tipo 33/TT12, but the chassis flex was a significant issue. So it is not possible to say that 'that chassis is not stiff enough, it can't win', but it is possible to say 'the reason they are so far ahead of us is due to their ultra-stiff chassis'.

PITCH OPTIMIZATION

In Chapter 2 we discussed hydro-pneumatic suspension. One of the key benefits of the system, and indeed Leyland's hydragas, was the optimization of pitch, meaning that the front and rear of the vehicle would work in harmony. The cleverness came from the fact that front forces were fed to the rear to equalize the movement of the chassis. So even a speed bump would be traversed without the uncomfortable see-saw motion on springs and dampers.

However, springs and dampers can be pitch optimized – but only for a nominated speed. As the front axle hits a bump it creates an upward force in the suspension, partially absorbed by the spring but still moving the body upwards. The rear axle will soon start the same movement, though how soon depends on the length of the wheelbase. However, by increasing the frequency of the rear suspension, it is possible to time the movements of front and rear so that they both finish at the same time.

The equation that governs this is relatively simple. The pitch-optimized speed (V) is governed by a multiplier (3.6), and the length of the wheelbase (L) divided by the difference between front and rear frequencies (f).

Obviously the longer the wheelbase, the higher the rear frequency needs to be to 'catch up' with the front. The other side of the relationship is that the lower the chosen speed you wish to pitch optimize the chassis for, the higher the rear frequency will have to be. There would come a point where an unaccep-

MG Rover hydragas system on an MGF, showing the car body staying flat whilst it traverses an uneven road.

$$V \, (km/h) = 3.6 \, \frac{L}{\dfrac{1}{f \, front} - \dfrac{1}{f \, rear}}$$

Pitch optimization formula.

table trade-off in comfort for rear-seat passengers prevents pitch optimization at low speeds. However, this is indeed the reason why a small city car often tends to feel very stiffly sprung when you are in the back seat. A city car will tend to be pitch optimized for a lower speed because its natural environment demands low speeds. Conversely a racing car travelling at high speeds is likely to be pitch optimized to the average or top speed that it may see.

There is conflict in this area, and the author has read numerous opinions to suggest that many people do not believe pitch optimization is important in racing vehicles. But if you ring team managers for comment, you'll be unlikely to get the answers you are looking for. It is clear this is something you'll need to be addressing designers and race engineers about, and quite rightly race teams and manufacturers guard it as their most precious commodity. More often than not, the information you obtain will lead to a range of opinions, covering a range of likely scenarios. Picture a longer wheelbase that may add aerodynamic benefits: could that not mean that the pitch optimization requires too high a rear spring rate?

Part of the reasoning is that in a rear-wheel-drive vehicle, increasing the frequency of the suspension will reduce traction. Increasing the frequency will work the tyre harder and reduce body roll. But does it always reduce traction? There is a school of thought that talks about mechanical grip, and the influence of stiffer springs reducing grip. The reality is that there will be a spring rate that is ideal for maximum grip on a given surface. On tarmac it is the tyre and chassis capability that will define the amount of spring rate that is required.

There is an argument that if the tyre were particularly sensitive towards its limit, then running higher rear frequency than the front might overwork the tyre, and cause a loss of grip as it overheats. Generally speaking, because the desired pitch optimization speed is relatively high for racing, the rear suspension doesn't need a much higher frequency than the front. There is no real sense in not trying it as a starting point. Then ideally the chassis can be balanced front to rear using the anti-roll bars.

There are examples where front-wheel-drive cars will run much higher rear frequencies than would be normal, simply to achieve mobility of the rear axle, used as a tool to dial out understeer.

The objective of this book is to help you in your endeavour to improve your vehicle's handling, and pitch optimization is something to be heartily recommended. In terms of deciding what speed to optimize for, the suggestion would be the average speed around a course for a small and light car, particularly a front-wheel-drive car. For high-powered rear-wheel-drive or mid-engined vehicles, the increase in rear suspension frequency can be reduced by opting for a pitch speed closer to a higher average speed.

One of the challenges when developing a vehicle is trying to assess what the real suspension frequency is. Stripping down the complete suspension system, weighing components, and taking measurements of critical points of the suspension is often made difficult because of the shape of the components and the angles involved.

Some readers will want to understand their vehicle suspension without getting their hands dirty. This is often possible without removing a wheel by taking some photographs and some key measurements (measuring springs will usually require the vehicle be raised). You make assumptions for unsprung weight and use a formula to make an estimation of the spring rate, without actually removing it and getting it measured. This task is enough for you to understand the car's suspension frequency and the speed it is pitch optimized for (though it may not be pitch optimized).

The original idea was to obtain the actual spring rates and motion ratios from the manufacturer, and compare them to the estimated measurements. Unfortunately, even after ownership was confirmed, Jaguar were unable to supply the actual spring rates, motion ratios and pitch optimization speed. As a flip side to that, Aston Martin recently rebuilt a new version of one of their old models from the old plans. Jaguar was owned by Ford at the time, so perhaps the information is classified.

The speed the standard car was pitch optimized for is found by looking at front and rear frequency and then using the formula, which takes into account the wheelbase. In the case of the Jaguar it is approximately 42mph, possibly a little lower than one would imagine the original design was specified for, but it certainly explains why the car rides so well and the rear feels as if it is working in harmony with the front.

After stripping the easy weight from the vehicle, including replacing the two seats with those from a focused Hot hatch, the S-type tipped the scales at 1,461kg. As a comparison, a Golf R weighs 1,521kg,

and that is its published kerb weight, not service weight. The service weight on a log book gives a better indication, with all operating fluids on board.

The change in weight mainly occurred on the rear of the car once it was sat back on the scales. The front/rear split is now 55.8 per cent front, and 44.2 per cent rear. The pitch optimization speed has reduced to just 28mph, as proportionately the rear axle has gained more stiffness, up from 1.48 to 1.70Hz (whereas the front has only gone from 1.21 to 1.22Hz, mainly due to weight of the engine and box, and most of the weight loss being behind the centre of gravity). The car is likely to be a little wayward at the rear due to this change.

Stage two will be working out what wheel rates are required to give 2Hz on the rear, with the equivalent front rate for a pitch speed of 70mph. 1.69Hz on the front axle with 2Hz on the rear is 70.8mph. This will require a wheel rate on the front of 244lb/in (4.36kg/Fmm) and on the rear 261lb/in (4.66kg/Fmm).

It is possible to calculate the spring rate (SR) required with the formula shown in the picture below.

So this will require a 572lb/in front spring (10.21kg/Fmm) and a rear spring of 692lb/in (12.36kg/Fmm). If this rear spring sounds huge, don't forget the motion ratio difference, and that the rear needs to be stiffer than the front if the chassis is to be pitch optimized.

It is worth remembering that as you take out more weight from a vehicle (for example for a race car, front bumpers and rear bumpers can be lightened, perspex windows, and a composite boot and bonnet used) the suspension will rise and the spring frequency (stiffness) will increase. It therefore makes most sense to remove as much weight as possible before designing your suspension rates.

$$SR = \frac{WR}{(MR)^2 (ACF)}$$

Formula to calculate spring rate required for a given wheel rate.

Pitch Optimization – Not Every Manufacturer Tries

For every person looking to optimize their suspension for outright grip on a tarmac circuit, there may well be just as many who would give their right arm for more travel and compliance in their suspension. Such is the appalling nature of many roads in the United Kingdom, combined with the never-ceasing industry desire for a larger wheel and a skinnier tyre, that compliance has become the new nirvana.

When Balance Motor Sport was asked to help make a Skoda Superb 4×4 Estate better handle unsurfaced roads, to more quickly attend the needs of farm animals, the initial thought was that this wasn't very motor sport. The driver's husband, however, had been given a challenge to fix the car's inherent weakness over such surfaces. Balance Motor Sport were willing to try and help, and the challenge was accepted.

He'd tried to find an off-the-shelf product but none seemed to exist. Most garages only want to fit product that is available. If a lift kit doesn't exist for a vehicle, then arguably most places won't want to develop such a solution.

Mindful of the fact that the brief was to keep the cost down, a suggestion of custom coil springs to raise the right height approximately 35mm, matched with standard dampers rather than custom units, was made. As you raise a vehicle up, you increase the available compression travel but reduce the amount of rebound travel. This is why the amount of lift was kept to a sensible level, as running out of droop travel on unsurfaced roads wouldn't be helpful. In addition, geometry change on the rear axle with too much lift will become unfavourable, necessitating specialist parts to bring it within limits.

The first step of the job was to take a set of measurements of the car's suspension to work out the motion ratio front and rear. This vehicle uses the ubiquitous (within the VAG group) MQB platform. Sporting a front MacPherson strut-type suspension, the front motion ratio is minimal, but of course due to the squaring of the ratio, still significant for calculations. On the rear the multi-link design has a significant loss ratio which, when squared, makes it actually quite difficult to achieve a reasonable wheel rate without an very high-rate spring. Given that pitch optimization requires a higher rear spring frequency than the front, you would have expected a big spring

Skoda Superb top mount featuring bolts 'the wrong way round'.

to be fitted. Somewhat unusually, the rear spring gives a lower spring frequency than the front. Perhaps the logic is that – given this vehicle is designed to offer a comfortable ride – over a long wheelbase with a high loss ratio, an excessively high-rate spring would have been required to pitch optimize the chassis.

Whatever the manufacturer's thinking, it's sometimes wise not to reinvent the wheel, particularly when you're relying on the standard damper and you know that its parameters will be set to a certain spring rate. Move too far away from the standard rate and you could run into trouble with a mismatch of spring and damping rates.

What the rear spring does feature is a large amount of preload in order to keep the vehicle body afloat with such a low rear wheel rate.

A custom set of springs was designed, the objective being to increase the ride height by using a higher rate without resorting to a longer spring, as it was felt that installation issues could occur if the spring was too long.

The job threw up some challenges and we can now work through it in brief to see how it went.

(continued overleaf)

The lengths you need to go to in order to remove the damper: first the hub and brake assembly must be removed, as well as the anti-roll bar droplink and tie-rod end.

As the bolts for the top mount go underneath into the wheel arch area they corrode, making removal very difficult. If you try using a socket on the other side it won't work as they've been fitted with an eight-sided nut!

ABOVE: **The replacement SKF top mounts wisely use a conventional captive hex nut, which seems to be more securely retained as well.**

The new SKF top mount ready for assembly to the new damper.

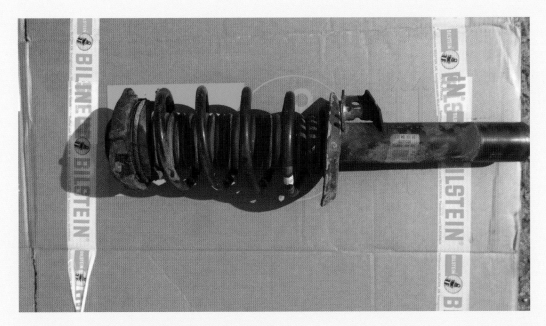

The original strut and spring removed from the car.

(continued from page 111)

Due to the design of the suspension, it's necessary to remove the complete hub assembly to remove the strut assembly.

Once all that is out of the way you'll need to undo the top mount nuts.

This is when you have a slight surprise, when you find that the VAG Group have decided that the internationally recognized mounting method for MacPherson strut tops is no longer suitable, and replaced with some downward facing fixings.

On the face of it, this would seem to be an over-reaction, as the nuts in the top mount are captive, and therefore it should be easy to remove the bolt. Unfortunately, because the bolt is exposed to the elements, it corrodes and does not want to come out easily. Pretty quickly you'll realise that the bolt is spinning because the captive nut is no longer captive. You might be thinking you could get a socket on the other side as it feels like there is a nut there. Then you'll notice that this nut you couldn't get a grip on is actually sporting eight sides instead of the regular six. The more sides a nut has, the more likely it is that it will round off. Were eight sides chosen to flummox the mechanic, or to provide more space to work in a restricted area?

Whatever the answer to this question it's interesting nonetheless the world-renowned SKF brand chose to opt for a six-sided captive nut on their replacement top mount.

Another interesting point to note is how inexpensive these mounts are; perhaps someone else has had this problem...

Once the old strut is removed it's time to get the new strut, spring and top mount assembled.

It's not always necessary to replace top mounts. In fact, if there is no noise or play and the bearing race is smooth, why change something that has life left?

With this design, though, the chances are you are better off getting a pair of mounts ready, as the bolts are unlikely to come free from the captive nuts after many years of service. Another option would be

(continued overleaf)

ABOVE: **The new Bilstein B4 strut assembled with the custom spring and new top mount.**

The custom rear spring installed with the new Bilstein B4 damper.

The finished job with its new higher ride height ready to tackle unsurfaced roads with gusto.

(continued from page 113)

to check you've got that eight-sided socket set for removal and perhaps replace the old nut with a hex nut. It's intriguing that there are two spheres of car maintenance, depending on available funds and ingenuity levels.

The new Bilstein B4 dampers are assembled with the new custom rate springs. These springs are made to Balance Motor Sport specifications by a Sheffield-based manufacturer, to give the required increase in ride height.

On the rear of the car, due to the mechanical loss ratio of the suspension, the spring is long and requires the arm to be dropped down to a fairly significant angle. Ideally it would be possible to use spring compressors; in this instance the room is limited and the compression required significant enough to rule out most compressors.

Take extreme care if using methods with a jack or load transfer that don't employ a spring compressor. Once installed you'd never know the springs free height was so great !

After installation the next step is to check everything twice to make sure nothing has bene missed. A good pointer to remember, is that this VAG MQB chassis is very similar across a wide range of models, so once you get used to their quirks, it will help across a very broad range of cars.

The next step is wheel alignment. You will notice on most cars that as you raise them the front will toe in and the rear will toe out. It's important to ensure that the alignment is set within sensible limits. Large changes in ride height up or down will require significant adjustment. A number of aftermarket manufacturers can help with alignment solutions.

The end result is best validated by the feedback from the owner: 'She's very happy with the results so far, comfort in corners and at speed significantly improved, first impressions just driving it home were great. I think the turning circle is tighter, or seems that way. Importantly, clearance and ride height is stable when loaded and much improved, which in turn leads to more confidence on farm tracks.'

SUSPENSION GEOMETRY: CAMBER

Camber angle is the degree of difference between the wheel's vertical axis perpendicular to the surface the wheel is on. This is why measurement of this angle, and any others, should be conducted on a flat surface. The majority of vehicles will have a camber angle close to zero degrees, which leaves the tyre contact patch in direct contact with the surface, and will maximize traction.

Looking at the diagram for positive and negative camber, one could be forgiven for thinking that an angle of zero will always result in the best contact patch and therefore grip, because in a static position both positive and negative settings have less contact patch in contact with the surface.

The problems occur when corners are thrown into the equation. Whatever purpose a vehicle is used for, only proper assessment of dynamic behaviour can lead to improvements. The fundamental problem is that as a vehicle rounds a corner, the loads move from the inside tyres to the outside tyres, and even if the suspension design does not lose any camber during this weight transfer process, the tyre itself will deform. What then happens is that the contact patch is not interacting with the ground as effectively. The outside edge of the tyre heats up, and increasing vertical load gives less lateral adhesion, and loss of grip occurs (see the feature box in Chapter 2 'Tyre Grip versus Vertical Load'). Tyre manufacturers test tyres using sophisticated machines and largely empirical models to generate the data at different camber and slip angles.

What the vehicle engineer must do is compensate for the tyre deflection by changing the camber angle. This can be done statically, by compensating with a fixed amount, or dynamically, by engineering the camber change into the suspension system. Even at the highest echelons of motor sport, a static negative camber setting is the norm, and this in some ways shows the challenges that even the best tyres present engineers. If you take a look at a modern Formula 1 car, you will see this.

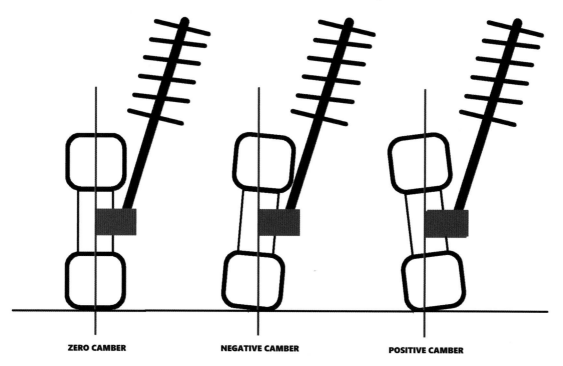

ZERO CAMBER   NEGATIVE CAMBER   POSITIVE CAMBER

Illustration of camber angle.

Different tyres require different camber settings, but it is usually the case that tyre load data is mysteriously difficult to obtain. Thankfully Avon tyres have a much more progressive attitude, and if you are building a race car they make enough data available for you to design your car's performance around the tyre.

By looking at the load data of the tyre, you will be able to ascertain the optimum working level of camber at the required dynamic load. If you have trouble visualizing this, consider a MacPherson strut suspension, which has a wheel rate that is very close to the spring rate. Imagine a simplified example, where the wheel rate is 300lb/in and the static weight is 300lb, and there is no preload, then that vehicle will compress the spring 1in as it is taken off the jack. If you knew that under heavy cornering, 300lb of vertical load from the other tyre could pass from the offside tyre (at this point the car could be visibly on two wheels, depending on the roll centre location), then the spring would compress a further inch. What then happens to that tyre with 600lb/in of vertical load? Tyre data could describe the tyres' response at various slip and camber angles. If the MacPherson strut suspension lost a single degree of camber under this vertical load, but the tyre data showed that the optimum angle was X degrees, then the difference between the actual dynamic camber and the tyres' optimum would be the required change to the static negative camber.

Chassis engineers will try to solve this engineering challenge in a production car without resorting to a high negative camber setting. The reason for this is that for the majority of its life a typical road car rarely experiences lateral G-force of more than 0.5g, where the loads are mainly vertical (including those from braking and acceleration). Having a static setting would impact on braking and accelerative forces, which is unacceptable in today's vehicles of high power and high weight.

When racing comes into the equation, compromises must be made, as corner speed is the most important aspect of pace around a typical circuit. This is from the perspective of tarmac high grip surfaces – negative camber is less of a worry, when high lateral loads are precluded by a loose surface. Typically, on a radial racing tyre, negative camber of up to 4 degrees will see a greater performance ratio between lateral load and vertical load. Often this means that a static setting of 2–5 degrees may be necessary, depending on the suspension design. This is almost a law across a wide variety of machinery. Switch to a cross- or bias-ply racing tyre and you may need as little as 1 degree.

CAMBER: A DIFFERENT WAY?

The following content and pictures turn almost everything said about camber on its head.

William F. Milliken (born 18 April 1911, died 28 July 2012) was a famous engineer who, like the best, learned from his mistakes and went on to achieve success at an even greater level, rather than giving up when it all went wrong. He is responsible for the seminal text *Race Car Vehicle Dynamics*. His background in aeronautical engineering led him to take the exacting standards required in that sphere into the automotive world. He developed new models, studying the tyre and chassis in innovative ways, and these have stood the test of time to such an extent that his text is the one you are most likely to find any top race team using as a reference.

In 1967, after approximately seven years of hard work, he tested his MX1 'camber car'. Looking at the picture it looks 'all wrong'. However, the most important aspect is the type of tyre he used: they are motorcycle tyres, not car tyres. They are therefore designed to work across a wide range of angle relative to the road surface. If you commute on a motorcycle the tyre will wear flat and make cornering dangerous.

The MX1 was notable for facilitating running at extreme angles of negative camber. To the naked eye it almost looks as if it wouldn't work, and indeed initial attempts would not drive in a straight line, due to camber thrust. Additional caster was found to be the cure. Milliken looked at the extreme angles that motorbikes generated, and the downward thrust that generates the grip at these angles. The MX1 was effectively two motorcycles – one for going left, and one for going right.

He found the optimum angle of 22 degrees would generate significantly higher G-forces – by around

The Milliken MX1 'camber car', showing the extreme levels of negative camber.

25 per cent – than was typical of the tyres of the day. Recent trials of this vehicle with modern tyres showed near 30 per cent improvements, and there would possibly be much more to come if development into his technology were more active. But thanks to an automotive enthusiast called Dean Butler, the car was recommissioned and has appeared more than once at the Goodwood Festival of Speed.

Mercedes-Benz (at the time Daimler Chrysler) made similar claims for the F400 Carving, which forty years or so later appeared to offer something revolutionary.

Mercedes F400 Carving active-camber concept car of 2001 – on the move, showing the camber change in action. DAIMLER AG

This concept car from Mercedes-Benz made its debut at the Tokyo Motor show in 2001. Looking at this car in a static position, there is no hint of the fiendishly clever suspension design beneath.

The F400 features 'active tyre tilt control' (ATTC) technology. This technology enables the front wheel camber angle to change by up to 20 degrees for greater cornering grip. Much like the Milliken camber car, special tyres are used to generate greater grip at extreme camber angles. Thanks to the active camber control system the car can generate significantly higher lateral forces – in the range of 30 per cent higher than a conventional car. Clearly this depends what car you are comparing it to – when the F400 Carving was made, the McLaren Senna had not turned a wheel.

It also deployed, under licence, the Citroën hydro-pneumatic suspension system, known by the Mercedes-Benz abbreviation 'ABC' – 'active body control'. It incorporated many other technologies that are familiar today, such as carbon fibre together with drive and brake by wire.

The reason that the independent wheel control of camber was important is that the outside and inside wheel have differing requirements for their contact patch as they round the corner. The outer wheel will need more negative camber, and the inside wheel may not: in fact it may be better off with positive camber. This is why, when modifying, a compromise must be struck.

GAINING MORE SPEED WITH NEGATIVE CAMBER

It is unlikely that you'll be modifying a vehicle with some form of active camber control, nor will you be using a motorcycle tyre. In addition, it's also somewhat unlikely that the load data you want will be available for your tyre. If you're running a bias-ply tyre like the ACB10, then you will need very little negative camber due to the side wall stiffness of the tyre.

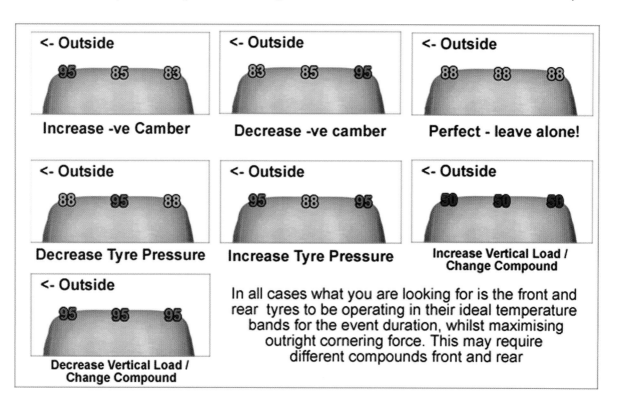

Tyre temperatures. BALANCE MOTORSPORT

Typically, most radial tyres will perform better with more dynamic negative camber, which usually has to be served up by a greater static setting.

Without all the data required, you need to obtain your own. This is best done by running some form of telemetry (even a modest GPS option on a mobile phone is better than nothing), and then also gathering data on tyre temperatures. Utilizing a degree of common sense, or referring to a diagram showing what to do with the data, will enable you to make adjustments that will lead to increased speed.

The most likely outcome is that the outer edge of the outside tyre will be running too hot, and the answer to the problem is more negative camber. Another likely outcome is that the temperature is too high or too low overall, indicating that the vertical load needs to be decreased or increased (perhaps by changing anti-roll bar stiffness), or that the tyre compound is too soft or too hard for the purpose.

In an ideal world you would be able to see what was happening to the tyre temperatures as you were driving, and this data would be logged. Devices now exist that cost a lot less than a pair of racing camshafts, so arguably this is a wise investment and should be thought of before trying to add more power.

That said, most will wait until you arrive into the pits to check the tyre temperatures. Naturally, the data will vary depending on the proportion of right and left turns, and the severity and speed of these corners. Although this might seem a little like fishing in the dark, the technique is proven and will enable you to set up the car for various different circuits, given enough testing time. In rather the same way as spark-plug readings, you need to get back to pits as soon as possible, since a 'cool-down' lap would take away the data clues. With the spark-plug reading you cut the engine straight after the event you are trying to read. So the idea with camber settings is to work with data and testing to understand what the tyre is giving you. There is no point equalizing the temperature across the tyre 10 degrees higher if you find, through G-force readings, that it is actually generating less grip. If a tyre is overheating in general across its width, then the chances are that this is due to too great a vertical load, rather than incorrect camber.

CASTER

Caster is the angle in relation to a vertical axis through the steered wheel. Although its effects on the contact patch may not seem as apparent as with camber, it has a definite and distinctive impact on handling. Many years ago, before the advent of power steering and high power engines and high performance tyres, cars used to run very little caster angle – in fact some would run negative caster to make the steering lighter. Caster angle appeared in an 1896 patent from Arthur Krebs, in which he said that caster was...:

> ...to ensure stability of direction by means of a special arrangement of fore-carriage, that is to say, to re-establish automatically the parallelism of the two axles of the vehicle when there is no tendency to keep them in any other direction, or after a temporary effort has caused them to diverge from said parallelism. ...The axle of the fore-carriage is situated a suitable distance behind the projection of the axis of the pivot pin in order to ensure the stability of direction above referred to.

The best way to visualize his statement is to think of how the steering behaves in your car after you have rounded a tight corner. You allow a light grip on the wheel to let it turn back to centre. If the wheel didn't want to return naturally to the centre point, it is easy to imagine how difficult a car could be to drive. So one of the key aspects of caster is its ability to provide straight-line stability.

CASTER AND TRAIL

Caster and trail are two different things. You may have heard someone mention a shopping-trolley wheel as a means to identify caster. So if caster provides stability, why does a shopping-trolley wheel – often called a caster wheel – sometimes move around of its own free will? In fact really it ought to be called a trailing wheel, not a caster wheel, because this type of 'caster' wheel actually has zero caster but a lot of trail.

Positive caster makes the pivot point of the steering scribe a centre line that is in front of the tyre

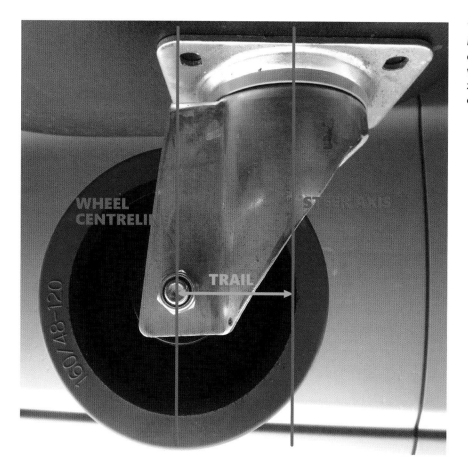

WHEEL CENTRELINE

STEER AXIS

TRAIL

160/48-120

This type of wheel is commonly known as a caster wheel, when in fact it has zero caster but a lot of trail.

contact patch. This distance is referred to as trail. The reason that positive caster is added is to provide a self-centring effect to the steering. This is why the shopping trolley has zero caster but does have significant trail. The objective is to allow the wheel both freedom of movement but also no directionality. However, clarity regarding these intertwined factors is not easily obtained, so it is best to study further what at first seems simple.

Caster alters the pivot point of the steering in such a way that the line between the pivot and the centre of the contact patch is intersected ahead of the contact patch. Trail is the difference between the steering centre line and the tyre contact patch, and is a side effect of a caster change – but as the steering axis does not have to pass through the wheel centre line, it can be set independently.

An interesting way of considering the difference between trail and caster is to understand how a

shopping-trolley wheel can wobble a little, particularly when it has seen a great deal of active service. It is following the direction of travel, but with no caster angle it does not favour straight-ahead movement (for the opposite situation consider that you could ride your bicycle with no hands thanks to the caster in the bicycle forks).

Positive caster also has trail, but it damps the oscillation. By adding caster angle to trail, another phenomenon is apparent, and that is caster's ability to provide straight-line stability via its lifting motion. As you turn a wheel with positive caster it provides a lifting effect to that wheel – this is why increased caster makes the steering heavier to turn,

Trail angle is very useful for enabling the driver to detect where the tyre is on its vertical load versus slip angle graph. Naturally the driver isn't thinking about a graph as the car loads up round a corner, so he relies on the feedback coming through the steering: too little trail and the car does not communicate back through the steering as it reaches the limit of grip, while too much trail can make the car seem so linear in response that it fools him into thinking there is more grip available than there really is. It does this by masking the pneumatic trail of the tyre.

Manufacturers will seek harmony between trail angle and caster angle to suit the application and tyre choice. You will need to optimize caster and trail in the same way. For example, world rally cars run a lot of trail, caster and compression travel to enable the driver to traverse difficult conditions at very high speeds; however, a single-seater racing car will need much less caster, trail and travel. The best strategy for modifications of trail and caster is to look at the drive layout and traction requirements first.

A front-wheel-drive hatchback, where dramatic increases in horsepower are going to be delivered,

will benefit more from increased caster and trail. Typically on a MacPherson strut-equipped vehicle the modification of choice is more caster through the use of an eccentric top mount, or a mount that has adjustable sliders to reposition the centre point of the strut.

Other designs increase caster by using a modified control-arm bushing. How this looks depends on the plane in which the bolt travels, but there will be some form of offset.

Whiteline is a trusted brand originating from Australia which produces a range of offset bushings to optimize caster. When the control arms have the bush mounted in the horizontal plane with the bolt running horizontally, the bush will be offset to enable the arm to move inwards at the rear mount position.

RIGHT: **Caster adjustable control-arm bushing.** WHITELINE UK

Front control-arm rear bushing changing caster and lift and dive geometry. WHITELINE UK

Front control-arm rear bushing that adds caster; this bush mounts with a vertical bolt. Notice the cut-out voids to permit control-arm movement. WHITELINE UK

ANTI-DIVE AND ANTI-LIFT GEOMETRY

Anti-dive and anti-lift geometry is used to control pitch movements on the front and rear axle by angling the control arms to intersect and create an 'anti' effect. Without some form of anti geometry the vehicle will lift on the front end and squat on the back end under acceleration, and vice versa under braking. Most vehicles will therefore use a percentage of lift and dive geometry. This is defined by the intersection of the tyre contact patch via the instantaneous centre, as it passes through the vertical from the centre-of-gravity height to the ground. It is usually defined as a percentage – 100 per cent means that the intersection occurs at the centre of gravity.

Like so many elements of the overall design, there is no definitive right or wrong for anti geometry. With reference to the diagram, it is easy to see that increasing the angles, and making the intersection occur earlier, will raise the anti properties on front or rear. How much is required for a chassis will depend on a number of factors, not least the spring and wheel rates, the acceleration and braking forces. For example, typically under braking for a corner,

as the front dives, this will lower the roll centre and potentially increase oversteer on corner entry. Having anti-dive geometry can therefore offer better roll-centre control.

Don't consider for a moment that more is necessarily better. Too much anti geometry in front or rear can interfere with the wheel control over bumps. In fact some of the after-market 'anti-lift kits' actually increase lift and dive in order to enable the suspension to work more freely over bumps. This is particularly important on a bumpy, high brake-force corner entry.

The answers probably lie in the range of 10 to 30 degrees, but an off-road race car may have pro-dive geometry together with very long wheel travel. If you read further into this subject you'll appreciate that this two-dimensional modelling is rarely suitable to describe what is happening dynamically when the vehicle is driving at speed. Two-dimensional force lines and intersects can quickly move around vast distances, so really a lot of the anti subject is somewhat academic. If you were building a race car, this is an area that should occupy less of your time than the equation relating to camber curve versus lateral grip.

FRONT   REAR

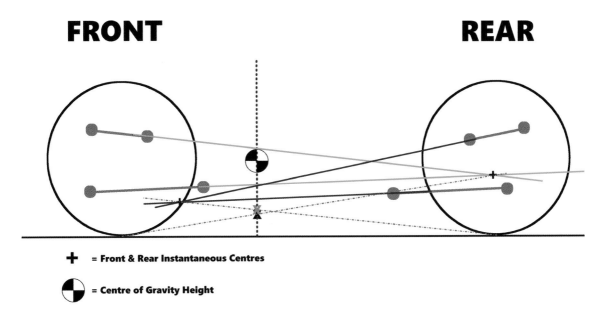

✚   = Front & Rear Instantaneous Centres

◓   = Centre of Gravity Height

Diagram showing how anti-lift (front) and anti-squat (rear) geometry can be defined.

WEIGHT JACKING

Weight jacking in the chassis occurs as a result of steering a wheel with positive caster. As the wheel is turned and the downward force of that wheel occurs, something happens to the chassis balance. As you round a corner, weight will transfer to the outside wheels. Positive caster can therefore have a favourable effect as it loads the inside wheel when you turn. This then increases the corner weight on the diagonally opposite wheel. So you are adding load to the lightly loaded inside front tyre, but increasing load on the rear offside tyre. This is weight jacking in action. Positive caster appears to give us the best of both worlds – not only straight-line stability, but at larger steering angles, increasing the rate of turn.

It might help here to look at how the kart uses caster angle. On a racing kart we may see up to 20 degrees of caster angle. This is because the kart runs a solid rear axle and needs to unload the inside rear tyre to get round the bend – otherwise it just wants to push (run wide and understeer). The kart will run around twice as much caster as a car, but the set-up parallels are similar to the car, just a bit more subtle because you tend not to have a fully locked differential on a car and of course you have suspension on a car.

It is therefore possible to suggest the following:

Add more power – more caster, particularly FWD and 4WD
Wet conditions – more caster
Tracks with tight corners – more caster
Tracks with fast corners – less caster

Of course these can't be rules or laws due to the complexity of chassis set-up – however, as a rule of thumb they are very helpful.

The astute among you will have noticed that sudden reference is made to more power requiring more caster. So far the discussion has been about stability and weight jacking – however, caster has other, desirable effects. It is the trail in the caster that gives more traction. As you add power this creates a downward force on to the tyre because it tries to lift the weight of the vehicle. You can try this with a shopping trolley wheel. It rotates easily one way but much less easily in the other direction. Modern cars use far greater caster angles partly as a result of power steering and stiffer chassis, but also due to the increasing power and torque of modern turbo-charged engines.

DYNAMIC NEGATIVE CAMBER

Caster isn't done yet – it has one more trick up its sleeve. This is the effect known as dynamic negative camber, which is the change in camber angle with steering angle. As you steer with positive caster, the outside wheel gains positive camber. The opposite happens on the inside wheel.

This effect can really help on a tight twisting circuit, as it gives the negative camber when needed around a tight corner but doesn't have the downside of a high static setting with regard to braking and acceleration traction.

Although the set-up information based on caster is simplistic, it is true that too much on a high speed circuit could make the car unstable in a turn, and too hard to turn.

Like most aspects of chassis tuning, there is a sweet spot. Although caster seems to give so much, eventually you run into the law of diminishing returns, and too much starts to affect overall grip negatively. This is mainly a result of the optimum tyre loads, meaning that less weight jacking would give more grip. A reasonable figure for a maximum would be about 10 degrees.

Arguably, a front-wheel-drive vehicle will benefit more from a high caster angle than a rear-wheel-drive vehicle. If the rear-wheel-drive vehicle has a locked differential (effectively like a kart with a solid axle), then the additional caster should prevent corner entry understeer.

STEERING AXIS INCLINATION AND SCRUB RADIUS

Steering axis inclination (SAI) has long been called 'king pin inclination'. Although very few modern vehicles now use a kingpin to facilitate steering, they are

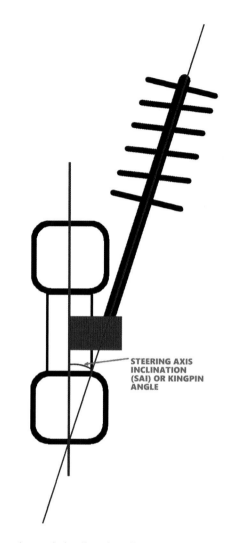

Steering axis inclination (SAI), or kingpin angle.

STEERING AXIS INCLINATION (SAI) OR KINGPIN ANGLE

still present on racing karts. In essence, the kingpin is a vertical pin, which is allowed to pivot inside its housing by way of a bearing top and bottom. The angle that this is set at, with reference to the vertical axis, is known as king pin inclination. However, due to kingpins being so rare on modern vehicles it is now more widely known as SAI.

SAI is generally employed with the primary purpose of reducing the scrub radius. Scrub radius (or 'king pin offset', as it is sometimes called) is the distance between the tyre centreline and the SAI (extended downward), as they interface at 90 degrees to the road surface. Somewhat oddly, in contrast to camber, SAI angle is referred to as positive when camber would be negative.

If the points meet at the contact patch, then this is known as zero scrub radius, though sometimes it is called 'centre-point steering'. This was first exploited commercially by Citroën in about 1949 with their A Series cars. However, true centre-point steering can only be achieved if there is also zero trail, and most cars will have some caster and therefore some trail.

The idea of centre-point steering is that by eliminating the scrub radius and trail the steering is lighter, more precise, and doesn't kick back. However, it may lack feel. There is an additional safety benefit under braking. If you have a positive scrub radius, and one front brake fails, then under heavy braking the remaining brake will create a strong torque in relation to the size of the scrub radius. This will be felt at the wheel. In the event of an accident it could be strong enough to cause injury to the wrist and arm, particularly if the wheel hits a solid object. So SAI is employed to ensure that the scrub radius is minimized.

Another effect of SAI is self-centring of the steering. This is because by inclining the steering angle, it causes the steering assembly to rise and fall as the wheels are turned. This effect, unlike caster, is the same on the left and right wheels. As the wheels are turned, SAI tries to push both tyres down into the road surface, and increases positive camber on both wheels.

This is not an effect that is needed in a performance vehicle, as adding positive camber will overheat the outside edge of the tyre – although on the inside wheel this positive camber gain helps. Somewhat confusingly, SAI is positive when the line is in the same plane as camber being negative, so a negatively cambered wheel is in at the top, but that same set-up will have a positive SAI.

You may wonder why an oval saloon race car has such an extreme amount of negative camber on the front outside wheel. This is partly due to the fact that the inside wheel is gaining favourable positive camber as a result of the SAI angle. There would be no point in adding static negative on the inside wheel, as it

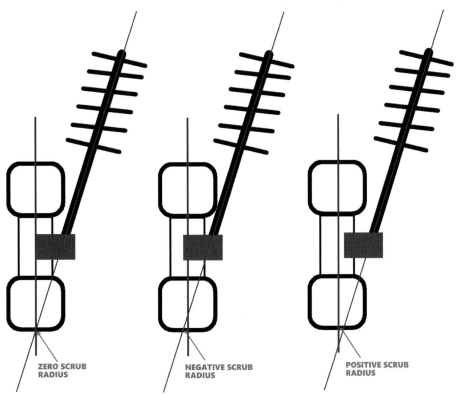

ZERO SCRUB RADIUS   NEGATIVE SCRUB RADIUS   POSITIVE SCRUB RADIUS

Diagram showing the scrub radius.

would get less grip when running clockwise. If you are only travelling clockwise or anti-clockwise, you can skew the set-up. If you have to go left and right, then balance is the key.

An extreme example of positive scrub is a kart. Most of the time these are equipped with only a rear brake, so the braking forces that the scrub angle creates are not an issue. However, on a gearbox kart there are brakes fitted to the front axles, and because the wheels are so small, there is no opportunity to arrange the geometry to minimize scrub. The impact of this is most obvious when braking: in a car you will tend to trail brake into a corner, but in a gearbox kart this technique doesn't work due to the brake reaction with the scrub radius.

So we have identified that positive scrub is unwanted, but it is worth understanding situations where it can change. Changing the offset of the wheel to a lower ET figure will change the scrub radius,

as will the use of wheel spacers. (ET is an abbreviation of the German word *Einpresstiefe*, which literally translates as 'insertion depth'.)

THE IMPACT OF WHEELS ON SCRUB RADIUS

The following diagram shows the difference between positive and negative offset. Most wheels are positive offset, meaning that the mounting face of the wheel is further inboard. The offset is usually described by an ET number.

By changing the centreline of the wheel, the scrub radius is altered. A very common modification is to fit wider wheels with a lower ET figure. This will change the scrub radius. Note that fitting a wider wheel, and keeping the ET figure the same, will not change the scrub radius, although clearance may be an issue.

The negative effects of positive scrub can be wheels prone to wandering and tramlining, a reduc-

———— **Wheel Centreline**
---------- **Wheel Mounting Surface to Hub**

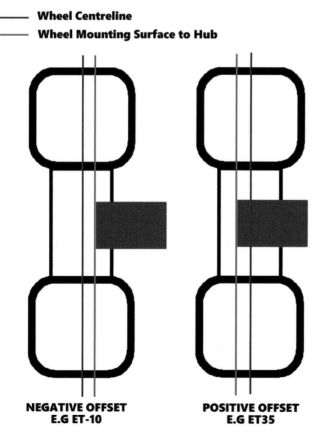

**NEGATIVE OFFSET
E.G ET-10**

**POSITIVE OFFSET
E.G ET35**

Diagram showing the wheel offset.

tion in wheel rate, and also, especially when used with a limited slip differential, plenty of torque steer. (For a RWD vehicle the torque steer factor is not relevant.)

NEGATIVE SCRUB

The majority of modern car manufacturers work hard to try and implement a small negative scrub radius. The aim is to provide the feedback that positive scrub provides, without the inherent safety issues that positive scrub comes with. Although zero scrub is appealing, having no torque reaction to a bump can make the steering seem 'disconnected' – hence the current trend for a small amount of negative scrub.

Something that makes this harder to achieve is the growth in larger SUV-type vehicles and large, high-powered cars, both of which need bigger brakes to stop as quickly. Trying to package the brake and hub sufficiently far into the wheel to give a negative scrub radius is not easy. Some manufacturers have adopted a dual pivot-point design, which has two separate radius arms connecting to the hub in different positions. Conventional set-ups for both strut and double-wishbone suspension will have only a single ball joint and will pivot around that axis. The dual pivot point makes it possible for the vehicle manufacturer to achieve the minimal negative scrub they desire, whilst also permitting the use of larger brakes. The dual pivot design enables the steering-axis pivot point to be nearer the centreline of the wheel, even if a wheel with a lower ET figure is used.

Another factor compounding too much positive scrub is the fitting of very wide, low-profile tyres with too much negative camber, due to the effects of the loads and slip angles being different across the contact patch. In addition, the inside and outside of the contact patch are describing slightly different arcs as they round a corner. As a result, the camber thrust, together with the variations in tyre grip, can cause the vehicle to wander and shimmy, particularly under power with a torque-biasing limited slip differential. Narrower tyres with more cross-sectional area reduce this tendency.

BMW dual pivot design found on the F20 to F36 models, with two control arms attached to the hub with two separate ball joints.

ACKERMANN ANGLE

Ackermann geometry is designed to reduce the slip angles that tyres must follow when forced to round a corner. The outside wheel is travelling at a higher speed around a larger radius than the inside wheel. With no Ackermann angle then each wheel would receive the same amount of steering angle. By moving the steering arm connection behind the steering pivot point, the inside wheel will turn at a larger angle in relation to the outside wheel.

Although the phenomenon is named after Rudolph Ackermann who filed the patent in 1818, Erasmus Darwin could have laid claim to its invention, as he manufactured such a linkage for his own horse-drawn carriage in 1759. In fact Erasmus was a bit of a pioneer, as in 1779 he also sketched an oxygen-hydrogen rocket in a manner that would not be seen for another one hundred years.

However, cars are not designed with pure Ackermann. As it doesn't take into account the dynamics and all the forces at work, pure Ackermann can only be suitable for low speeds.

How much Ackermann is required depends on a lot of factors, but a good 'ready reckoner' is that if you take a stock city car and try and turn it into a 300HP racing car, the stock rack will more than likely have too much Ackermann. Ackermann has a fairly minimal effect at small amounts of lock, so in high speed and very wide radius turns the stock rack should be all right. However, as lock increases, particularly at the high slip angles associated with racing tyres, then Ackermann increases also. This usually results in the inside wheel being 'oversteered' in relation to the vertical load on the tyre and the optimum slip angle.

This, then, is the 'key' to Ackermann setting: it needs to be tuned too. The use the vehicle is put to, and the tyres it is using, will decide what level of Ackermann, if any, is required. Some may even end up with the Ackermann angle reversed so the outside front wheel is gaining more lock. If this heavily loaded tyre could take a larger slip angle and generate more load as a result, then potentially anti-Ackermann will work.

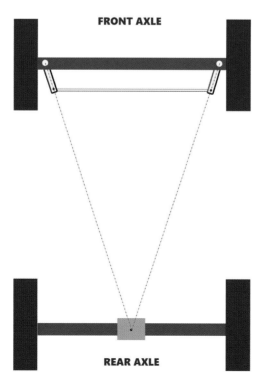

FRONT AXLE

REAR AXLE

A diagram showing perfect Ackermann steering, where the steering arms coincide with the centre of the rear axle.

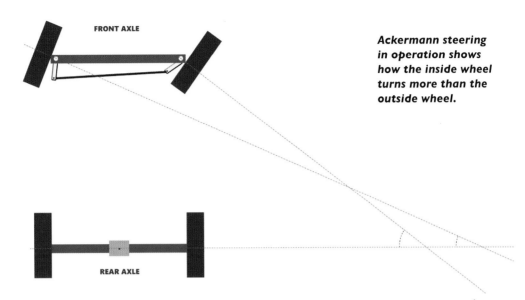

Ackermann steering in operation shows how the inside wheel turns more than the outside wheel.

INCLUDED ANGLE – SAI AND CAMBER

Included angle is, as its name suggests, more than one angle. Technically an included angle is where two lines meet at a common point know as a vertex. A combination of SAI and camber does just this, and it can be very useful as a diagnostic aid, to show if something has got bent out of shape. For example, if camber were out by a small amount on either side of the vehicle, this would not necessarily be a cause for concern – if, that is, the SAI angle were the same. If the SAI had increased and the camber had increased, the included angle would increase. What the operator of the alignment machine is looking for is divergence from the norm.

The included angle is obtained by adding positive camber or subtracting negative camber from the SAI angle. It is here that you might spot that camber and SAI are measured inversely. Negative camber is in the same plane as positive SAI. So as you lean a strut inwards towards the centreline, you gain negative camber and positive SAI.

You might wonder how often strut casings get bent to cause this problem. In fact it is common in rally and rallycross, but can show up on road cars as

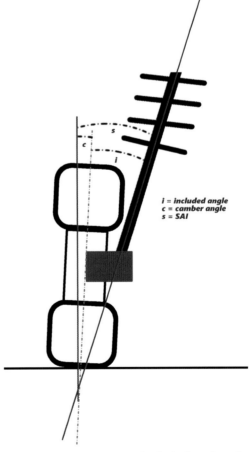

i = included angle
c = camber angle
s = SAI

The diagram shows how included angle takes into account both camber and SAI angle.

well. A combination of high speed and very uneven surfaces could well be enough to bend a strut casing, and cause an anomaly of included angle.

TOE ANGLE

Toe angle is arguably the simplest to understand, and the easiest to write about, and yet arguably it is the one that has the most impact for the average motorist and racing driver alike. Simply expressed, it is the angle off from the dead ahead for both the front and rear axle. You can either have toe-out (a negative figure) or toe-in (a positive figure).

Historically, front toe was set according to whether the vehicle was driven by the rear or the front axle. The effect of power to FWD wheels would tend to make them toe out – so some degree of static toe in was specified. Nowadays, the static toe setting is more a function of how the manufacturer finally optimizes the chassis for the customer. For example, look at the Alfa 147/156, which has a front toe setting of 0.28 degrees with a tolerance of +/- 0.13 degrees. The tolerance alone is much more than the toe-out setting provided by many makers overall.

Toe-out works by effectively changing the dynamic Ackermann angles. Ackermann seeks to ensure that the inside wheel scribes a tighter line than the outside, while toe-out on turns can provide more mid-corner grip by simulating the effect of Ackermann. It also can generate more heat in the tyre in a straight line, and more tyre heat can equal more grip, particularly in a sprint event where there are very few laps.

Too much toe-in can make the steering seemingly adopt a life of its own, and generally limits grip in the turns. As always the compromise must be found based on the conditions, the car, the tyre and the driver.

ROLL STEER AND BUMP STEER

These two elements of geometry are subtly different, but both deal with the steering reaction of a wheel as it moves through compression and extension. For the purposes of simplicity we will assume that bump steer also refers to the effect of roll steer.

Typically modern cars will tend to steer outwards under compression and inwards on extension on the front axle, while the opposite would normally be true of the rear axle. The logic here is that it will create understeer, which nearly all vehicles are set up to do on the limit. Granted there are notable exceptions – for example in certain torsion-bar Peugeots and Citroëns, where a strong passive rear steer effect meant that lifting off can cause a large oversteer moment.

It would be useful at this point to clarify this when discussing bump steer, toe-in and toe-out as the terms we want to use. If we use the term 'oversteer' we are talking about the handling attitude of the whole vehicle. In actual fact the oversteer could result from an *understeering* rear axle.

Manufacturers have to work hard to ensure that their vehicles are safe under a wide range of conditions. They need to be safe when heavily loaded up to the maximum axle weight, and indeed beyond for that extra layer of security. With the driver able to move weight around the vehicle dynamically, it is important that the vehicle doesn't possess dangerous handling traits by having an 'incorrect' bump steer set-up between front and rear.

The reason they make the front outside wheel toe out under compression is to gently make the car understeer at higher slip angles. This lets the driver know when the tyre is overloaded. The inside front wheel is now steering inwards, which also contributes to the front axle steering away from the desired axis. On the rear the opposite is happening, and by toe-in under compression the outside rear tyre is trying to push the car to scribe a tighter line than the steered angle. In reality at high levels of slip the car is always moving away from the steered axis on both axles. The idea behind bump and roll steer is to design in safety rather than make the vehicle a dangerous drive. However, many arguably dangerous designs still made production in the earlier years of the industry.

High-level jet-fighter aircraft, which use fly-by-wire, are deliberately designed to be unstable so they can make tighter turns and be more manoeuvrable. This might seem counter-intuitive, but with the modern avionic computer systems available they are able to present this unstable device to the pilots with no inherent flaws or indeed instabilities. These kinds of flight control system need to work flawlessly and have back-up systems in the event of failure. It is a harmony of computer power designed to make a plane better than one without a computer. However, at Farnborough International Air show the author has witnessed the most spectacular air displays by Russian jets without fly-by-wire, so having a computer isn't essential. One wonders how much more skill is involved in flying a cutting-edge plane that doesn't have fly-by-wire.

Car design is a somewhat different field as there are no immediate threats from enemy fire. The modern design solutions seek to engineer in inherent safety. However, this throws up opportunity, and if we look at the jet fighter as inspiration, by changing the bump steer we can engineer more front and rear grip.

If the bump steer is reduced on the front axle to close to zero, the driver will tend to find that the front end generates more turning force for a given amount of steering input. In addition, on limit grip is increased as the tyre is able to operate at the optimum slip angle and vertical load for maximum grip.

On the rear axle one has to be more careful. Although generally referred to in disparaging terms, the live axle does have an advantage with regard to bump steer, in essence as the two wheels are rigidly stuck together on the axle. It is neither greatly affected by bump or roll steer. Other systems may have quite a large degree of toe-in under compression. Up to a point this tightens the line of the rear end of the car, preventing oversteer. However, as the loads are increased due to the difference in slip angle and steered angle, grip will eventually be lost.

A good case in point is the trailing arm design on the BMW E30 Series and the E36 Compact. Often severe uncontrollable oversteer can result, particularly under power and also under heavy braking (where it is then toeing out due to the rear rising). This often results in a spin. Too much rear toe change, then, is undesirable for high performance handling;

however, toe-in under compression is such a key safety feature, there may well be significant gains to be made by keeping it under tight control in the field of racing.

ROLL CENTRE HEIGHT

The roll centre is a notional point which can be drawn. It is a result of the instant centre of rotation, and is constructed by looking at the angles between the ball-joint pivot point and the inner control-arm mounting and the upper mounting plane. On a MacPherson strut suspension the upper arm is replaced by the top mounting so the angles can go wrong much more easily. At the point where these intersect, a line is drawn back to the centre of the tyre contact patch.

The SAE (Society of Engineers) definition of roll centre is force based: 'The point in the transverse vertical plane through any pair of wheel centres at which lateral forces may be applied to the sprung mass without producing suspension roll.' The roll centre determines how the weight moves around the chassis as lateral and longitudinal loads are applied. The front and rear roll centres are a roll couple, and work together based on the position of the centre of gravity in the chassis. This it is often referred to as the 'centre of mass'. The two are usually interchangeable with regard to chassis dynamics.

During cornering, when the roll centre is high, more weight is transferred via the control arms to the hard points of the vehicle. When the roll centre is low, then more weight is transferred via the springs.

VEHICLE DYNAMICS MODELLING

Bump steer and roll steer are an important element of the overall understeer/oversteer balance of a vehicle.

Within roll centre two different definitions were observed, one geometric and one force based – so why two definitions? Here we are starting to uncover part of the complexity of vehicle dynamics. There are different theories and different conventions, and ISO standards may differ from SAE. However, it is clearly

example Bundorf Analysis	FRONT	REAR
Load transfer effect and cornering stiffness of tyre	7.00	6.00
Aligning torque	0.20	-0.20
Roll camber	1.00	0.00
Roll steer	0.50	-0.30
Fy Compliance steer	0.32	-0.10
SAT compliance steer	0.75	0.60
Total Axle Cornering compliance	9.77	6.00
Total Axle Cornering compliance FRONT minus REAR (+ve understeer, -ve oversteer)	3.77	

Example of a Bundorf analysis.

vital at the highest levels of design to have data that is quantifiable and workable.

In 1976 a paper was written by R. T. Bundorf and R. L. Leffert called 'The Cornering Compliance Concept for Description of Vehicle Directional Control Properties'. It seeks to simplify the very complex physics at work with a front and rear compliance figure (denoted by Df and Dr respectively). The analysis takes in the following attributes:

Load transfer effect and the cornering stiffness of the tyres: During cornering the load transfer across the tyres generates varying slip angles and lateral grip versus the vertical load. Different tyres respond with different levels of grip. Friction theory says that the lateral grip should equal the downward pressure. In reality the maximum horizontal force (Fy) is related to vertical load, but usually with a loss ratio. This is how downforce can give 'free' additional grip. In a racing kart it is possible to generate significantly more lateral grip than vertical load, without downforce. Therefore it is best not to make assumptions about the 'typical' loss ratio. Safe to say, production cars without downforce on road tyres will tend to generate less lateral grip than vertical load.

Aligning torque: As well as generating lateral grip, the tyre generates an aligning force. When it is forced to turn, the structure of the tyre resists the force and naturally wants to return to its previous, unloaded state.

Roll camber: As the vehicle experiences roll, the kinematics of the suspension (the study of motion without referencing force – which is kinetics) will change the camber angle. This will usually vary, depending on the suspension design. For example,

with an unequal length, non-parallel, double wishbone suspension system, the engineer will be able to design in favourable camber change.

Roll steer: As the vehicle experiences roll, the kinematics of the suspension will change the steered angle of the tyre. This in turn creates a cornering force.

Fy compliance steer: The lateral force at the tyre contact patch causes the wheel to rotate about the steer axis, generating a steering angle.

SAT compliance steer: The aligning torque directly twists the wheel on the compliances in the suspension, generating a steer angle.

If you look at the Bundorf analysis pictured above, you can see that the positive values denote understeer and the negative values oversteer. Typically a vehicle is set up with more front understeer, and 'understeer' on the rear axle becomes whole vehicle oversteer. Generally speaking, most chassis engineers will seek the handling balance they want without having to increase any one area too much.

For example, one approach would be to decide on the suspension frequency required for the vehicle's operational environment and choice of tyre. Generally speaking, for a road vehicle springs will be fairly soft, so roll will be controlled by anti-roll bars, so these, along with the roll-centre height, would decide the chassis balance. Most of these studies would be done in a 3D modelling environment, so if the test data said the vehicle didn't have enough understeer, the engineer might use roll steer to change the understeer balance. However, too much roll steer will make the car steer itself on an uneven road.

All the elements of the Bundorf analysis can be used, but the objective should not be to use one element to an extreme. For example, dialling in understeer using SAT Compliance Steer will result in rubbery steering. Some cars have lifeless and rubbery steering by utilizing compliance bushes to change the understeer budget, but this is not a preferred route.

The ISO model looks at the following forces:

Fx – longitudinal force: force fore and aft, particularly braking and acceleration.

Fy – lateral force: cornering force.

Fz – vertical force: for example, the weight of the shell.

Mz – twisting force: the self-aligning force exerted by the tyre, into the direction the wheels are driving. This is important for getting the feel of understeer and oversteer, increased as velocity rises.

Now this isn't a book on vehicle dynamics, but the information to follow shows you just how complicated a field it is by highlighting both the SAE and ISO terms, and the different systems of measurement.

Thanks must be given to Michael Sayers, who wrote to try and harmonize these different systems and terms to provide a useful reference, in his piece 'Standard Terminology for Vehicle Dynamics' (The University of Michigan Transportation Research Institute (UMTRI), 22 February 1996).

TYRE AND WHEEL AXIS SYSTEMS

Earth-fixed coordinate system: *Coordinate system based on the earth-fixed axis system and an origin that lies in a reference ground plane*

Intermediate axis system (X, Y, Z): Right-handed orthogonal *axis system* whose Z axis is parallel to ZE, and whose Y axis is perpendicular to both ZE and XV. This axis system can be obtained by rotating the earth-fixed axis system about the ZE axis by the vehicle *yaw angle*.

Reference frame: A geometric environment in which points remain fixed with respect to each other at all times.

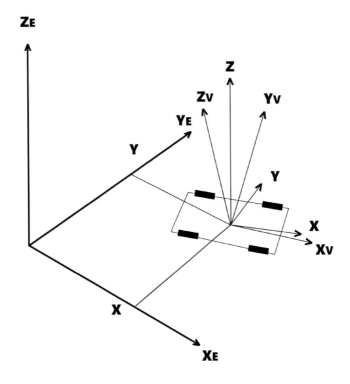

Earth-fixed vehicle axis system.

Road axis system (XR, YR, ZR): Right-handed orthogonal *axis system* whose ZR axis is normal to the road, at the centre of *tyre contact*, and whose XR axis is perpendicular to the wheel *spin axis* (YW). For an uneven road, a different road axis system exists for each tyre.

Road plane: A reference plane tangent to the road surface at the tyre *contact centre*. For an uneven road, a different road plane exists for each tyre.

Vehicle axis system (XV, YV, ZV): Right-handed orthogonal *axis system* fixed in the *vehicle reference frame*. The XV axis is primarily horizontal in the *vehicle plane of symmetry* and points forward. The ZV axis is vertical and the YV axis is lateral. The directions should coincide with the *earth-fixed axis system* when the vehicle is upright and aligned with the XV axis parallel to the XE axis. (*See* Figure 2.) (SAE, ISO).

Vehicle plane of symmetry: The lateral (XVZV) centre plane of the vehicle.

Vehicle reference frame: *Reference frame* associated with the vehicle body. It is typically defined to coincide with the undeformed body of the vehicle body structure

So after that, you probably feel that the vehicle dynamics are best solved by real-world testing and tyre temperatures. Well, you wouldn't be far wrong, as this is a work on repairing, rebuilding and modifying, and not designing from scratch. The dynamics models that are available are just that. By seeking to simulate actual behaviour in a design process, and simplifying what is actually happening, can be very helpful, but can also lead to designs that seemingly should work, but are not well received by the driver.

A lack of variables is an issue – for example having no inputs for limited slip differentials, electronic brake and steering aids, and active suspension. What the models do is try to simplify something very complex, but actually in doing so they are also complex and flawed. This is why, in reality, even the

most well developed cars may end up getting subtle set-up changes to springs, dampers and anti-roll bars after being driven by motoring experts.

UNDERSTANDING THE BASICS

What we will do now is try to simplify the whole sphere of vehicle dynamics – no easy task when you consider that many a thesis has been written about one small branch of the subject.

YAW

Let's look at yaw, which is the movement around an up-and-down axis, left or right. Think of high yaw axis rotation as oversteer. The yaw rate will rely on the interaction between the front and rear axles. If you had Bundorf analysis data you would be able to see whether the vehicle is likely to have a high yaw rate.

Yaw control is generally achieved by ensuring that the centre of gravity is ahead of the centre of the wheelbase. If this is the case, yaw is damped and stiff. The term 'damped' is used because the effect of yaw damping is much the same as that of a damped spring. However, if the centre of gravity is behind the centre of the wheelbase, then at a certain speed the damping will become negative, and instability will result.

Referencing the image, the front axle is located *a* metres ahead of the centre of gravity, and the rear axle is *b* metres towards the rear from the centre of gravity. The body of the car is pointing in a direction θ (theta) while it is travelling in a direction Ψ (psi). In general, these are not the same. The tyre treads at the region of contact point in the direction of travel, but the hubs are aligned with the vehicle body, with the steering held central. The tyres distort as they rotate to accommodate this misalignment, and generate side forces as a consequence.

From directional stability study, denoting the angular velocity Ω (omega), the equations of motion are shown in the following diagram.

The coefficient of yaw damping is expressed as shown in the diagram opposite.

It is called damping by analogy with a mass-spring damper, which has a similar equation of motion. By

*Diagram to illustrate
the yaw dynamics of
a vehicle.*

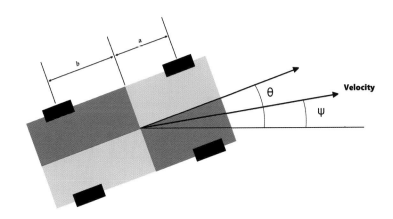

$$\frac{d\omega}{dt} = 2k\frac{(a-b)}{I}\beta - 2k\frac{(a^2+b^2)}{VI}\omega$$

*The equations
of motion, from
directional stability
study, denoting the
angular velocity* ω.

$$\frac{d\beta}{dt} = -\frac{4k}{MV}\beta + (1-2k)\frac{(b-a)}{MV^2}\omega$$

$$\frac{d\beta}{dt}$$

*Coefficient of
yaw damping.*

$$V^2 = \frac{2k(a+b)^2}{M(a-b)}$$

Equation to find the speed above which a vehicle will be unstable in yaw, when its centre of gravity is behind the centre of the wheelbase.

the same analogy, the coefficient of β will be called the 'stiffness', as its function is to return the system to zero deflection, in the same manner as a spring.

The form of the solution depends only on the signs of the damping and stiffness terms. There are four possible solutions:

1) Negative stiffness, negative damping = statically and dynamically unstable
2) Negative stiffness, positive damping = statically unstable
3) Positive stiffness, negative damping = dynamically unstable
4) Positive stiffness, positive damping = statically and dynamically stable

The fourth solution is what you want in a car – if the centre of gravity is ahead of the centre of the wheelbase the yaw damping will be positive and the vehicle will be stable at all speeds. If this isn't the case, then exceeding the speed given by the formula will result in instability.

It is easy to see why many just dismiss chassis work as 'a dark art' when presented with these kinds of equation. However, it is sometimes helpful when considering the advanced mathematics involved in vehicle dynamics, to appreciate how many intelligent people were involved to get to where we are today, and how long it took them. There is no need to fear the maths in these areas: if time is taken to study from literature aimed at beginners, it is relatively easy to understand the equations. One of the issues is that assumptions are made concerning the reader's knowledge of the subject, and many equations don't explicitly name all the variables, inputs and outputs, and axes.

If we go back in time to the era of Euclid of Alexandria – that is, fourth century BC – Euclid is often known as the 'founder of geometry'. His legacy was to establish that every point within a three-dimensional Euclidean space is determined by three coordinates.

It is surely a sobering thought that from these works from Euclid the study of the equations of motion (in physics, equations of motion are equations that describe the behaviour of a physical system, in terms of its motion, as a function of time) did not arrive for another 1,000 years!

This is a fascinating area of study and well beyond the scope of this work; nevertheless, the idea is to lead the reader to the source of the knowledge. When presented with a whole lot of equations it is all too easy to shut down because they are so inaccessible. This is why even the longest and most complicated papers will have a written summary that is more easily accessible.

The three-dimensional space of Euclidean geometry: a point in a three-dimensional space is a function of coordinates x, y and z.

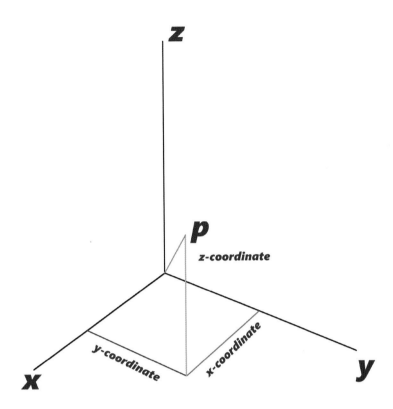

Galileo proved first that the path of a projectile is a parabola. He had an understanding of centrifugal force and gave a correct definition of momentum. He understood that momentum was key, but measured it only by velocity and weight, and did not consider mass – this was Newton's input, to look at the way gravity influences an object. Newtonian laws of motion allow the position and velocity of a body to be expressed dynamically as a differential equation. A differential equation relates a function to its derivatives (with reference to velocity, acceleration and various forces acting on the body). Some equations may be solved with a simple closed form. Other problems cannot be, and are therefore subject to computer simulation models to make approximate suggestions. Improvements to a model based on qualitative results will increase accuracy.

So to put it simply, if you can absorb the work of 1,000 years of mathematics, you may be able to understand fully the equations of motion that shape the way the suspension system works on a vehicle.

It wasn't until as recently as the 1960s that the pioneering works of Milliken developed and proved the automotive equations of motion. His work culminated in the extremely advanced TIRF flat-belt tyre tester. Interestingly it is with these models that some of the cracks start to occur. Pajecka was a master of engineering who developed the 'Magic Formula' tyre models, but ultimately, once you are on the limit modelling becomes much more difficult. It is more of an attempt to simplify and crystallize something that is almost unobtainable. At some point, when you go to the ultimate degree, you will see the data saying one thing but the driver saying something else.

Fortunately, salvation is at hand in the guise of the driver. If you study the equation you will see that the input velocity of steering angle, together with lateral acceleration, are very important factors. This is where the old adage 'smooth is fast' finds its foundations. A driver who works up to, and around, the mechanical limits that he discerns from feedback, is likely to be faster than the one whose aggressive inputs overcome the limits of the tyres and the machine.

It is interesting that in a conversation with the ever friendly Dick Bennetts from West Surrey Racing, we both came to the conclusion that no matter what science and history you put into the equation, sometimes the faster driver doesn't employ the 'on paper' faster technique. Take, for example, left foot braking, which should, from a time perspective, be quicker. However, what if the more rapid transitions between pedals actually compromised grip, and that a slightly slower transition yielded a faster result? It is certainly the case that there are exceptions to be found, as the textbook line round a corner can be very different from the real interface between tyre, car and driver.

CAMBER VERSUS LATERAL LOAD

Together with yaw, one of the most important aspects to consider for chassis balance is camber/ Fy stiffness − that is, camber and lateral cornering force. We have looked earlier at the importance of camber and its influence on the tyres' ultimate ability to generate maximum lateral force. Imagine the frustration of the automotive engineer who designs the vehicle around a specific tyre, to know that many of the replacement tyres fitted offer nowhere near the

performance of the original. And the owner fitting these also spoils the handling balance of the vehicle.

TOE VERSUS LATERAL LOAD

Toe change on lateral load (roll steer) is another key variable in the overall handling balance of the vehicle. Toe change is usually set with the front toeing out under load, and the rear toeing in. Different suspension designs have quirks that can cause very interesting on-limit handling. Part of the problem with turning a car into numbers using the various physical and empirical models, is that on-limit behaviour changes the 'rules', which up to that point were fairly consistent.

TOE VERSUS MZ

Mz is the twisting force, also known as SAT (self-aligning torque). It is the self-aligning force exerted by the tyre, into the direction the wheels are driving; it is the result of pneumatic trail multiplied by lateral force. Peak steering torque is measured by lateral force multiplied by mechanical trail plus pneumatic

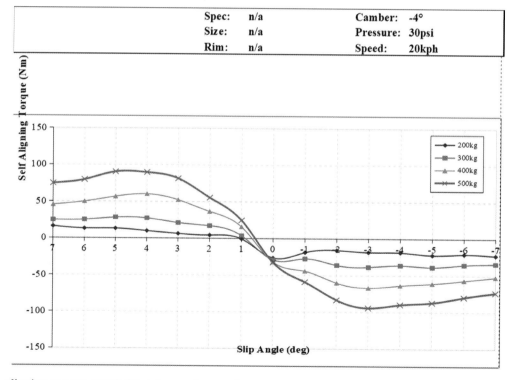

Self-aligning torque graph (Mz) for an Avon saloon-car race tyre.

trail. It is possible to set the mechanical trail in a wide range, and there are no real right or wrong amounts as long as there is enough to create some kind of torque. Otherwise you lose a very valuable way of discerning when the limits of grip are nearly reached.

Different tyres change the toe/Mz compliance, and this is a source of potential risk when a car is developed around a superior tyre, only to find that something completely different in quality and performance is fitted as a replacement. Tyre manufacturers may make available a graph for vertical load as discussed earlier, but also self-aligning torque, as illustrated.

In a discussion with Dave Joy, a motor-sport design engineer at Cooper Tire (who own the Avon racing tyre brand), it was interesting to try and understand if race teams and drivers looked at SAT graphs to decide what impact they had on driver feel and feedback. Like so many discussions you may have with those more informed, it often comes down to the fact that the tyre is being tested on a steel rotating drum at 12mph (20km/h), and not in the heat of the moment on a race track. Whilst the modelling for load data will help the engineer specify the car set-up and particularly camber angle, it is just a model, and empirical data is usually more valuable.

KINEMATIC SUMMARY

If you took the time to model your car – or if you were lucky enough to have access to the manufacturer's chassis engineers – then you might find that a summary of a vehicle's kinematics is as follows:

Compliance characteristics of the front axle:
Bounce stiffness: 37 [N/mm]
Roll stiffness: 52 [N/mm]
Lateral stiffness: 1.9 [kN/mm]
Toe angle due to lateral force (toe-out): 0.28 [deg/kN]
Longitudinal stiffness: 0.3 [kN/mm]
Toe angle due to longitudinal force (toe-out): 0.625 [deg/kN]
Steering stiffness: Mz0.0025 [deg/Nm]

It would make life much easier if this information were freely available, not just for the production car on which you wanted to base your race car, but also for all the modifications that were available (for example, a bump steer kit). Unfortunately this is not the case, so you'll end up following an approach driven by change, test and change again until you get the result you want. Or you'll start a quest to learn much more about chassis dynamics, and model your next project from the start.

THE IMPORTANCE OF DAMPING

To understand the importance of damping, take a look at the highest echelons of motor sport, and witness the similarity in suspension design, and the widespread use of control tyres. Then, when you look at four-way dampers and you realize the multitude of set-up variations that these give you, it is easy to see why dampers are the icing on the cake.

UPGRADING DAMPERS – WHAT TO CHOOSE?

If you've jumped straight here from Chapter 2 you'll know that we have already discussed the different types of damper available, from the cheap, twin-tube non-adjustable type, right up to a sophisticated four-way mono-tube unit.

So what will you choose for your project? If you are competing in some form of motor sport, the regulations may well state what you can and can't use. This might be a blessing if the specified damper is a sealed unit, as you might then be able to assume that everyone is competing on a level playing field. However, other regulations may allow significant freedom, and this could make you think that you need to spend as much money as possible on the most sophisticated system. As with so many of the elements that we have discussed so far, it is about selecting the right solution to the problem, but also about seriously developing what you have, even if seemingly little adjustment is allowed.

Choosing the correct damper will therefore very much depend on what you have already done with your vehicle, and what you intend doing with it. Let's use a handful of examples to make things easier. Car One will be a road rally vehicle, of standard production, using OE specification components. Car Two is a modified production saloon, and Car Three a single seater.

Car One will hopefully be on the application list of Bilstein dampers, made by Thyssenkrupp, a very large German industrial company which bought the Bilstein damper company in 1988. It is now a wholly owned subsidiary called Thyssenkrupp Bilstein. They are clearly the largest producers of mono-tube principal dampers, and the pedigree dates back to the De Carbon dampers used on the Lancia Fulvia rally cars. Bilstein acquired the design, and the rest is history.

These distinctive yellow-coloured dampers (although Mercedes-Benz B4 units and a handful of others are also mono-tube but black in colour) nearly always employ the mono-tube design and are an excellent upgrade from the standard unit. Caveats apply, as sometimes Bilstein mono-tube may well be the original equipment damper, in which case the change from the black original equipment version to the yellow sport version will usually just be a change in valving and possibly length. In addition sometimes they make early production versions as a sport-valved twin-tube unit. This confusion aside, they are still a renowned producer of mono-tube principal dampers.

So Car One hopefully can take advantage of an off-the-shelf product that will lead to significant benefits in dynamic control. The larger piston size and high gas pressure of the mono-tube design will lead to better tyre contact with the surface and better body control.

Car Two is a fundamentally different beast, as modified production regulations usually dictate a great degree of freedom in suspension design, particularly the ability to move suspension pick-up points. As soon as you take the motor-sport genie out of the modified production bottle, you open up a realm of possibilities that can make this class of motor sport suddenly seem extremely complicated. Experience, on the other hand, teaches us that when a car is well

prepared and the basic design is good, it doesn't need four-way damping to be quick. There are so many factors at work in a chassis, that even the difference between mono-tube and twin-tube could be scarcely noticeable in the hands of an expert driver over a short distance.

When you get to Car Three the level of development in every area of design will be exaggerated compared to the modified production car. An independent three-way unit with a remote reservoir would likely be the minimum specification required. Throw in the aerodynamic downforce that the majority of single seaters employ, and the damper baseline just got even more complicated. Small changes can make a big difference to grid and race position when the field is more closely bunched together. The complexity of all the dynamics, and the skill required by the driver to interface with the engineer, probably point to why there are many notable examples of hill-climb racers who have designed, built, developed and driven their vehicle to success.

In single-seater racing formula there is usually a team of engineers working with the driver to deliver results. This is big budget stuff, and why at national hill-climb level in the United Kingdom the keen amateur can still reach the top level.

When you distil the mix of variables that you'll need to make a competitive car, you'd be forgiven for thinking that damping wasn't as crucial as many will suggest it is. But the reality is, that adjustments to damping can make significant improvements in lap time. This works largely on the assumption that everything else has been done correctly. If there is a fundamental issue with the understeer budget (the combination of tyre and chassis attributes that collectively deliver understeer to chassis) then no amount of damping adjustment is going to solve that problem. More empirically, a chassis with a negative Bundorf analysis is not the answer to a consistent race result, and damping adjustment can't fix this.

So let's assume the basics are all correct, and that you are faced with the choice between a budget adjustable kit and a kit costing many times as much. Will you go faster with the more expensive kit?

Could you set the cheaper kit to work as well as the faster kit? The answers to many chassis questions are based on other facts. For example, let's assume that you had a choice between a mono-tube single adjustable damper that was made from the highest quality components with a repeatable and adjustable dynamometer result from a variable shim stack. Then you had an option of a dual adjust that compromised on piston size, gas pressure and shim stack and dyno development. Which will be quicker? Arguably with the right engineering support the damper with high quality rebuildable components and single adjust will be quicker than the 'off the peg' twin-tube double adjust with no recourse to dyno development. The challenge is in finding the correct base setting.

SETTING THE DAMPING CURVE

Assuming you are to brief your damper manufacturer on what you need, they will want to know some key bits of information to specify a damper for you. The Penske form illustrated asks for the intended application, overall weight, corner weights, spring rate, unsprung weight, suspension motion ratio and angle correction (if the damper is at an angle there will be a loss in load).

On a visit to Penske Racing UK (SPA Design) a discussion on the challenge of developing a base setting for a vehicle was had with damper engineer Alex Ruggieri. With regard to the damper specification form he said:

As you can see, it is very basic information on the car, however it is enough to work out a valving that will control the spring and the car overall frequency. It is important to distinguish between estimated and preferred data, as that will change the approach of how we set the baseline on the adjusters. Estimated data will force us to give more range of adjustment on the damper, which means that clicks of compression and rebound will have more effect on the damping curve, therefore the precision for any single click will be reduced. The baseline will be set at the midway point to enable

the customer to find the right balance and leave enough margin for adjustment.

Once the baseline setting is known, the requirement for a wide range of adjustment isn't there. Arguably this applies to racing more than the extremes of rallying. But what if you know more than the base setting? Perhaps you've got a control tyre and have already established some peak G figures. Alex said:

If all information asked in the form is available, and the maximum G the car can generate is known, you can easily calculate how much force will go through the damper, as well as the maximum speed achievable (always considering situations that do not exceed the maximum G supported by the tyre). Usually at this stage, if the customer is able to know the G limits of the car, it means that they have access to a lot more information than us, even full kinematics models and CAD assemblies, so it is easier for them to give us exactly the target force/speed they want, to achieve the right balance front and rear.

Knowing the CG and Rc of each axle will allow you to calculate the speed of how the weight is transferred from side to side; then motion ratios, anti-squat and anti-dive geometries will allow you to find out the amount of force going through the damper. Knowing force and speed is the key for setting up a precise baseline.

When working at these levels (professional motor sport) it is important to know that the adjusters will play a very small role in the set-up of the damper. With the data available you set up the dampers at the right baseline, and only use the adjusters to tweak the curve based on track conditions, track temperature and tyre degradation tyre pressure. For each track you will probably have to re-valve the damper for the application as you will surely know the maximum G your car will be able to generate on that track, therefore a new valving can be worked out for each application.

Piston choice is all related to the above; usually with less information we tend to use the linear

Damper Spec Sheet

SPA DESIGN — **PENSKE RACING SHOCKS. UK**

Company Name		Date	
Company Address		Due Date	
		Telephone	
		Email	

Make	Model	Year	Aerodynamic Loads	Engine Position	Drive

Application					
Road	Race	Rally	Drag	Short Track	Other

Vehicle Specification

Overall Weight		Leave blank if unknown	If Estimated, circle 'E'	If Preferred, circle 'P'

Front Left

Corner Weight		E	P
Spring Rate		E	P
Unsprung Weight		E	P
Motion Ratio		E	P
Angle Correction		E	P

Front Right

Corner Weight		E	P
Spring Rate		E	P
Unsprung Weight		E	P
Motion Ratio		E	P
Angle Correction		E	P

Rear Left

Corner Weight		E	P
Spring Rate		E	P
Unsprung Weight		E	P
Motion Ratio		E	P
Angle Correction		E	P

Rear Right

Corner Weight		E	P
Spring Rate		E	P
Unsprung Weight		E	P
Motion Ratio		E	P
Angle Correction		E	P

Damper Information

Front

Open Length	
Closed Length	
Spring Hardware Size	
Ways of Adjustments	
Piggyback	
Remote + Hose Length	
None	

Rear

Open Length	
Closed Length	
Spring Hardware Size	
Way of Adjustments	
Piggyback	
Remote + Hose Length	
None	

NOTES

Damper specification sheet, courtesy of Spa Design/Penske Racing UK.

pistons or the high flow if the valving is very soft, but this is because it is better to use a slightly less restrictive piston with stiffer shims than the other way around. Other types of piston are used to achieve different curves than the linear piston, which would be difficult to get by using the shim stack alone.

To conclude, we do have access to some data from some vehicle manufacturers, so it becomes easy to work out the valving if we already know the base, and we end up adapting the valving to the driving skills of the driver and the kind of racing.

It is easy to see that Penske are operating on a different plane to the kind of products cheaply available on the internet. In order to construct a damper for a customer they will get the information they need from the customer completing a fairly comprehensive form.

Some assumptions can be made in this process. At the very least you are going to need to know corner weights, unsprung weight, motion ratio and damper angle, and if you recall, the angle correction factor is there in the formula to assess the effect on the spring rate of the damper angle.

MODIFYING AND ADJUSTING DAMPING CURVE

Alex alluded to the different pistons available. In the picture you can see the different piston types and the shape of the corresponding damping curve.

If you look at the linear piston curve, as its name suggests the damping force increases in a linear relationship with the damping velocity (in this car, inches/second). A linear piston is characterized by a high flow rate at low velocity. At high velocities the damping curve increases, so that the damper is able to assist the spring in high energy, high velocity events. A good example of this would be a gravel rally car or a rallycross car.

A linear piston will have a flat face on both sides. With the linear high flow piston, each piston face has a dished surface, to preload the valve shims flat against the piston face. The high flow piston ports are larger and allow for roughly 50 per cent more

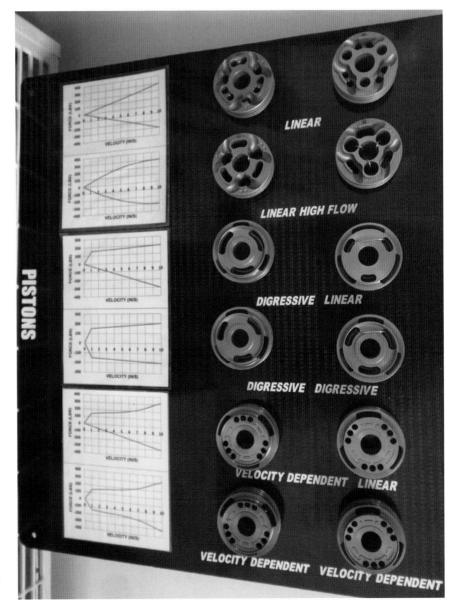

Penske piston options.

Penske dished piston, which facilitates shim preload.

flow. The result is a more compliant feel, which typically gives more mechanical grip but less support. The standard dishing is 1 degree on both the compression and rebound sides of the piston. By increasing the compression side dishing to 2 degrees, the shims become increasingly preloaded, causing a slight delay in opening during compression movement. The dishing causes the shims to 'snap' open, in return giving the car a 'snappier' feel as opposed to a smooth roll – once again this modification is for driver feel. This piston would be ideal on a fairly light vehicle competing on tight, twisty courses with plenty of left/right sequences.

A digressive piston is made possible by having a raised edge around the flow surface. This allows the shims to be preloaded. It's also possible to machine a digressive piston by having a concave face. A digressive piston has higher force rates at lower velocities than the linear piston. Conversely, at higher velocities, more oil flows through the piston and the damping force is lower. A digressive valve is generally a great choice for making a vehicle feel more responsive and sporty whilst enabling it to ride higher velocity events more smoothly. This generally translates into more control over relatively rough surfaces –

however, turn up the volume to rallycross level and a digressive piston will not have enough high speed force to cope.

A progressive piston is usually a modified linear piston which can introduce a damper curve that gets progressively stiffer but is usefully softer at lower velocities. This is ideal for certain off-road applications where you are perhaps climbing boulders or traversing craters. This can be achieved by shim-stack changes, bleed holes, and/or a low speed bypass.

A linear piston can be made to have a digressive effect by introducing bleed holes into the piston or via cut-outs in the shims.

A further type of piston used by Penske is the velocity dependent piston. This can be valved as a digressive piston, with the added benefit of being able to adjust the linear slope after the digressive 'knee' on both compression and rebound. This piston design enables the user to have maximum compression support and also maximum rebound control. This type of set-up is usually best on smooth, flat surfaces.

On the velocity dependent piston the low speed section is controlled by the amount of bleed, the outer valve stack configuration, and the amount of preload to determine the knee/nose profile. The digressive profile is set by the thickness of the outer stack. The amount of time that the curve stays digressive is also influenced by the stiffness of the inner stack, and when it is initiated is also controlled by the preload.

The linear values and profile are set by the thickness of the inner stack.

A double digressive piston has a digressive damper response on both the compression and rebound curve. Being digressive on rebound as well as compression lets the tyre get back in contact with the ground more quickly than a linear rate damper after a high velocity event. This could be very useful in a road vehicle trying to interact with, but not fight, the road surface.

Although damper design has developed over the years, it is arguably a mature market, and true innovation is now scarce. Many companies seeking to gain competitive advantage will give new names to a valve or piston technology, but if you look at the curve and the response they are achieving it is rarely groundbreaking technology.

The important thing to look at (assuming you've established that the very best materials are being used) is the curve. Then you need to try and translate that into the environment you are operating in.

It was interesting to compare the approach of Penske at the high end, with a multitude of different piston designs, with a relatively new player in the mono-tube market, Gaz Shocks, who use just a single piston design.

Gaz Shocks mono-tube piston rod assembly.

Gaz Shocks mono-tube piston – a linear flow type.

SHIM-STACK TRICKS

Although a number of different piston types have been identified, the shim stack itself is where the majority of tuning is conducted. The shim stack includes support, cover, bypass, bleed and preload shims, in a variety of thicknesses and diameters, particularly with a linear piston which, through the arrangement of the shim stack, can be given digressive, linear and progressive characteristics.

As we saw earlier in the Bilstein rebuild, the 'shim-stack worksheet' will dictate the size and shape of shims employed for a given damper.

FLUTTER SHIM STACK

A flutter shim stack is where the pyramid shape is broken by the use of a smaller diameter shim, which permits more movement from the shim above. It is usually used on the compression side, and by giving the largest shim the ability to move more, it softens the force of the damper by allowing greater flow through the compression port. The larger the shim that creates this effect, the softer the damper response.

RATE-PLATE SHIM STACK

The rate-plate shim has the opposite effect: it reduces flow through the compression shim stack. By using a much thicker and wider shim than usual – like a roof on the pyramid – the damper will produce a different rate at high velocities. For example, this technique could be used to make a digressive piston perform in a more linear fashion at high rates.

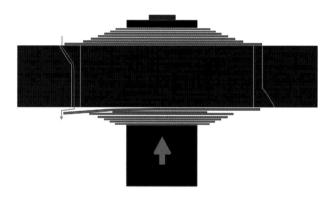

Flutter shim stack – compression movement – used to increase flow.

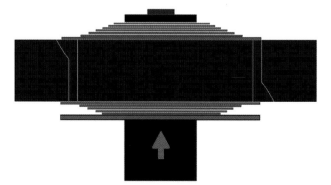

Rate-plate shim stack, used on a compression shim stack to reduce flow.

NOTCHED SHIMS

A notched shim can be used, and this will increase flow rate and change the curve characteristic (more flow = less force).

BELOW: *Penske notched shims.*

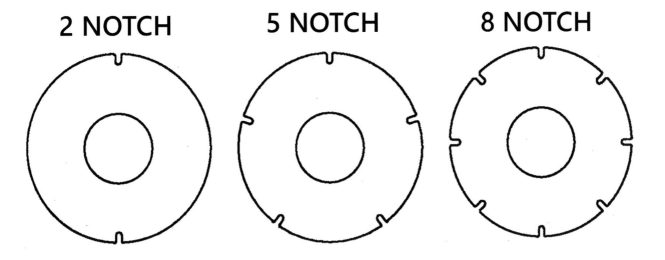

2 NOTCH   5 NOTCH   8 NOTCH

Penske Notched Shims 0.004 " shim (0.1016mm)			
Notches	Relative Flow	% increase	Equivalent Ø Hole
2	0.48		0.022
5	1.2	150.00%	0.035
8	1.93	60.83%	0.044

Penske notched shims specification.

DIY DAMPER TUNING

Earlier we saw how Bilstein rebuild their mono-tube dampers. They are designed in such a way that specialist equipment is needed to gas and re-gas the dampers. However, it is possible to find specialists who will retrospectively weld a Schrader valve on Bilstein casings, which would then enable you to de-gas and re-gas the damper. When you look at dampers available in the UK it is rare to see any with a Schrader valve. For example, the inexpensive Gaz Shocks mono-tube design uses a syringe style of gas recharge via a simple silicon seal – this is very similar in principle to a football needle used to push through the rubber seal, and is a cost-effective solution that prevents tampering to a degree.

Look across the pond in the USA, though, and the situation is very different. Although Britain possesses some extraordinary engineering talent, arguably at club level the American competitor is far more 'hands on' with their car. Witness the Penske damper – something of a phenomenon in the USA, but much less well known in the UK. In the UK they are viewed as a high end solution (which is true), and this is further reinforced when you establish that at the time of writing they are the currently control damper supplier in British Touring Cars and have seen success in F1, CART, ALMS, FIA GT and so on. And yet the Penske damper is often seen at club level in the USA, and the competitor will often service and rebuild his or her own dampers.

Although it is not clear if the UK market will ever follow suit, let's take a look at the rebuild of a Penske damper – the competitor could complete this procedure at home if they had a suitable nitrogen tank to re-gas the damper. One special Penske tool is all that is required to take the unit apart.

REBUILDING A PENSKE DAMPER

Firstly an oil catch tray is added to the damper. The damper is depressurized via the Schrader valves attached to the high-speed reservoir and piston. It is worth mentioning at this point that the Penske damper is quite unusual in featuring a full-size piston in the high-speed reservoir. This permits finer control

Gaz Shocks mono-tube gas seal.

Penske strip-down – add the oil tray to the damper.

*Penske strip-down
– depressurize the
damper via the
Schrader valve.*

*Penske full-size
high-speed piston.*

Penske strip-down – using the special Penske tool, undo the retaining nut.

Penske strip-down – undoing the shim-stack retaining nut.

of high-speed events, and has the added benefit of using the same type of shims fitted to the main damper.

Once the gas is removed from the damper, the guide bearing and retainer can be undone, again with the use of the special tool.

Next the piston rod is removed using the tool – at this point you can see the rebound shim stack on the top of the piston. If you are simply servicing you may well be leaving the shim stack intact, or shims may be replaced, owing to fatigue, with the same shape and size. Penske in fact recommend that for every thirty hours of track time, or annually, you should do the following: change the oil, replace the shaft seal O-ring, the wiper seal, the shaft-bearing O-ring, the reservoir cap O-ring, the piston O-ring, the floating piston quad ring and the valve shims.

This is certainly in stark contrast to the average motorist's expectation that his original equipment dampers might last for 50,000 miles (1,000 hours at 50mph) or more. However, in racing any small advantage is hard fought, and when you think how little time the tyres last, an annual damper rebuild doesn't seem too onerous. Serious teams using Penske dampers are able to have on-track support from the manufacturer themselves, and the main task of these damper engineers will be changing the shim stack to suit the circuit.

Naturally at this point, if a new set of shims is to be used, it helps to have a worksheet so that you can double check the size and thickness of each shim as they are assembled.

The piston on this touring car damper is the velocity dependent version, which enables a great degree of flexibility over the damper curve – by modifying the shim stack, piston jet and preload, just about any damper curve the engineer wants is available.

Penske strip-down – showing the large, notched rebound shim in place, which will permit more flow through the damper.

The Penske VDP piston shim stack combines a number of techniques to create this distinctive-looking shim stack. Used correctly, this can give the vehicle a number of advantages at different force, velocity and displacement events.

Should a shim stack change be in order, this will be the final stage before rebuilding the damper.

Once the shim stack is assembled for both compression and rebound circuits, the retaining nut is tightened to the specified torque and the damper filled with oil, then reassembled.

Once the guide/retainer is tightened, the damper is ready to re-gas. Care must be taken on assembly not to trap air in the damper.

Penske strip-down – with the rebound shim stack removed, the velocity-dependent piston is now visible.

Compression

Rebound

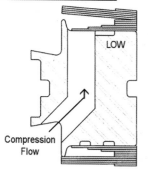
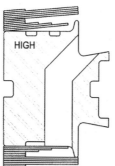

LOW | HIGH

Compression Flow

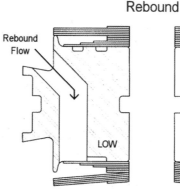
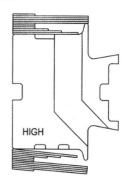

Rebound Flow

LOW | HIGH

This graph illustrates the way in which the two different circuits operate on compression.

This graph illustrates the way in which the two different circuits operate on rebound side.

Low speed works the digressive stack and high speed works both.

Penske velocity-dependent piston hybrid shim stack.

Penske rebuild – damper being reassembled after receiving the measured amount of damper oil.

Penske rebuild – damper being reassembled after receiving the measured amount of damper oil.

Penske rebuild – re-pressurizing with nitrogen gas.

Nitrogen gas at approximately 200psi is used. Different gas pressures and volumes are possible for different applications. In fact Penske offer a new approach to this, with a service to pressure balance dampers. They say:

Pressure balancing is done by measuring pressure at four different locations inside the damper and making adjustments to head-valve build, adjuster settings, main piston build, or a combination of all three to reduce internal pressures. Pressure tap locations are:

(1) Rebound side of the main piston (oil pressure) – between the shaft bearing and the piston

(2) Compression side of the main piston (oil pressure) – between the main piston and the head valve or CD housing

(3) Head valve (oil pressure) – on the exhaust side of the head valve between the compression shims of the head valve or the CD adjuster and reservoir piston

(4) Reservoir (gas pressure) – in the gas reservoir

By evaluating pressure levels at these locations versus time while cycling the damper at a constant velocity, a good picture of dynamic pressure changes results. A graph of pressure versus time gives one direction in tuning the damper components to balance the damper.

The objective is to reduce the hysteresis of the damper, which is the lag in response of the damper to an input. Furthermore, it ensures that the rebound side of the damper doesn't get close to 0 degrees, or even worse, create vacuum. If it does, this will cavitate the oil, and the damper response will worsen as the oil heats up and degrades. So by pressure balancing they are considering both the internal working pressures of the damper, and then selecting the gas charge to suit.

DYNO TESTING

Once the damper has been reassembled, the next step is to test it on the dyno. In the UK, Penske dampers are distributed by SPA Design, who are

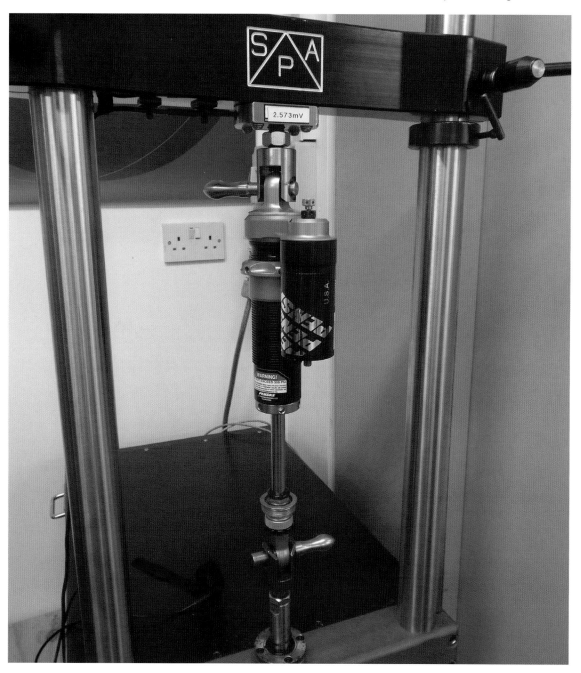

Penske rebuild – tested on the damper dynamometer.

also a world-leading producer of damper dynos. At first sight, a damper dynamometer appears relatively simple: the damper is connected to the dyno top and bottom, and when the dyno is activated, it works the damper through a compression and rebound cycle.

This is achieved via an electric motor and a crank, which turns the rotational movement of the motor into up-and-down movement. The reason that these devices are actually complicated and expensive is to do with the forces involved. Their entry-level model is aimed at the serious club racer (for now, mostly sold in the USA): it will produce a load of up to 1,500kg (3,300lb) and weighs 50kg, and is capable of peak velocity up to 0.28m/s (11in per second).

Moving up to the more serious but still worktop-compatible BTP4000, this can produce peak velocity of up to 1.32m/s (52in per second).

Different damper designers test their dampers at different speeds, and this can make comparison difficult. Bilstein, for example, tend to use a high-speed test velocity of 0.52m/s (20.5in per second). The SPA Club dyno wouldn't allow you to test at these high-speed frequencies. However, there is an argument to say that at these kinds of velocity other issues are coming into play, such as running out of stroke,

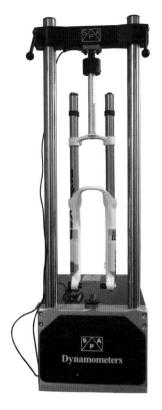

Spa design BTP4,000 damper dynamometer testing a pair of forks.

Alfa 155 at Snetterton driven by Giampiero Simoni: no more weight transfer can occur once on two wheels!

SIMON LEWIS
TRANSPORT BOOKS

and hitting the bump stop. Very high-speed events are beyond the effective control of most dampers, and in the cockpit it's a case of 'hold on tight!'. An example would be driving over heavy kerbing on a race circuit at very high speeds. This may result in a vehicle becoming unstable, and possibly two wheels will leave the ground (or more, if it rolls over!).

Seeing a car flying through the air as a result of a major compression event is perhaps more telling of the kind of forces the dyno needs to try and replicate than a number. In order to create such force from a relatively small electric motor (typically 3–4HP), a precision-engineered gearbox and sophisticated control equipment is employed in every SPA dynamometer. A reduction gearbox (just as a car employs) reduces motor rotational speed in return for more torque. This torque multiplication is what enables the 3–4HP motor to create a force of 1,500kg (3,300lb). This is amazing when you consider that the typical torque of the motor alone would only be 10Nm (7.38ft/lb).

Rally use throws up its own set of challenges. If you look online you will find many a video of a car that traverses a hump, goes airborne and then upon landing crashes spectacularly. A study called 'Vehicle Dynamics of a Jumping Rallycross Car' by Emil Sällberg and Robert Ekman in 2015 demonstrates that part of the issue is that the car rarely lands evenly on all four wheels. Very often it will land more heavily on one wheel as it experiences pitch and yaw whilst 'flying' through the air. Peak damper velocities in their study were shown to be as high as 3.02m/s; most damper dynamometers cannot get close to this kind of velocity.

However, the SPA BI99 stand-alone damper dynamometer takes damper testing to the next level – with motor options up to 7.5kW (10HP), the BI99 offers higher test speeds with higher force capabilities permitting advanced testing of dampers. Strokes can be configured up to 100mm, with a peak test speed of up to 2.89m/s. This is invaluable when trying to assess the performance of dampers at the extreme.

Although we know that a damper converts spring energy into heat, usually when we are driving a vehicle we are unaware of the temperature of the damper.

SPA design BI99 damper dynamometer.

When you see a damper on a dyno with the temperature of the casing being directly monitored, it is almost surreal to see how quickly the temperatures rise. SPA damper dynos come complete with a temperature sender, which ensures that changes to the shim stack and gas pressure are compared against the baseline at the same or similar temperature. As oil viscosity changes with temperature, it would be all too easy to send out dampers from a workshop with different valving in winter and summer due to ambient temperature changes. Next time you get a chance, take a note of how your suspension seems stiffer in the winter than in the summer.

In fact this is a clue to a fairly simple 'cheat' that can be employed. Most race series will try and control

Inside a damper dynamometer – you can see the heavy duty gearbox and motor control gear.

A Penske damper undergoing testing on a SPA dynamometer.

the choice of damper, to ensure a more level playing field. Where a control unit is specified in some series, it may or may not say whether you can make modifications to the damper. The general rule of thumb is, if it doesn't say you can do it, you can't. That said, there is no doubt that you will see on racetracks around the world two cars, both running the same package of standard parts, having wildly differing performance around the corners. One trick that some racers on a budget will do, is to change the oil viscosity to a higher figure. A thicker oil will flow less freely through the piston and shim stack, and therefore create more force for a given input. However, this is a very hit-and-miss approach to tuning a damper, and using an oil with too high a viscosity could cause failure of the damper.

In addition, the regulations are unlikely to be promoting a change in oil. Often dampers will be free up to a certain specification, enabling the driver and engineer a wide range of set-up options through external adjustment and/or re-valving. The use of oil of a consistent weight from a reputable manufacturer is the best way to ensure long term repeatability, and more importantly the acquisition of knowledge.

THE CHASSIS ENGINEER IS KEY

The acquisition of knowledge in damping is something that takes time. An engineer would most likely prefer to be working with a specific car, damper and driver over the course of the season on a wide range of circuits. Ideally they could then do the same thing the year after. Building up data for different circuits and ambient conditions and indeed different tyres could take years, but that experience can be translated into a competitive advantage. Let's say, for example, that in British Touring Cars, the car is performing well, but then it starts raining and the temperature drops, requiring a change of tyres and damping. The damping adjustment range is no longer ideal. It's the lunch break and you've got the damper engineer on hand. He can rebuild a pair of dampers in thirty minutes, so you decide to optimize the driven axle for traction by changing the shim stack. As the rain pours down, the way the cars drive out of the corners is far superior and enables a victory, where had everything been left as it was, a mid-table result is the best that could have been hoped for.

Even if a mid-event damper rebuild is beyond the capability and budget of the average club racer, it is common at the high end of motor sport.

A good chassis engineer isn't going to start trying to get their driver to understand complicated vehicle dynamics equations, nor are they going to try and get him to talk in equations of motion. What they will do is understand from the driver's 'seat-of-the-pants' feedback, as well as any telemetry and tyre temperature data, what needs to be changed to gain an advantage. The reason why a skilled chassis engineer is worth so much is that their knowledge and experience means they can make an effective change, and get it right first time. An inexperienced amateur on a budget could reasonably bring a damper dyno, different pistons and shims, and make changes at the circuit, but the likelihood of them getting it right first time is reduced due to their lack of experience.

In time, however, that amateur could go on to set up his fellow competitors' cars (for a fee, and, of course, assuming they were confident in their driving skills) – but in the top flight of motor sport any advantage a team has will be closely guarded. Note the F1 spying scandal in 2007, which landed McLaren a record $100 million fine. At the high end of motor sport, teams will sometimes break rules to get their hands on valuable data.

INTERPRETING DYNO GRAPHS

The software supplied with a damper dyno will usually permit two main types of chart. The first chart is plotting force against velocity, and usually looks rather like a ski slope or the side of half a mountain. The other type of chart is plotting force versus displacement at a known velocity, and looks more like a flying saucer.

The curves tell us different things, and different parts of their shape can be changed by making different modifications. The force versus velocity graph is arguably the easier to understand.

If you look at lower speed forces, these are the ones that affect the vehicle, largely in roll and over gentle undulations. As the velocities increase, the forces naturally do too. The high-speed forces would typically be generated by something like a kerb event or pothole. So let's take a practical example of how you could use the force versus velocity graph – if you had a race car that just couldn't ride kerbs, the chances are the graph would be very linear and very much a straight line from low speed to high speed. In this instance you could change the piston to a digressive one, and then re-dyno the damper to see what kind of reduction in high-speed forces you had achieved.

You can see how essential the dyno is to understanding the work of damper engineering. There is an old saying, 'You can't manage what you can't measure': this from Peter Drucker, an Austrian – and while we are on the subject of Austrians, Rudolf Hruska was the lead engineer on the Alfasud, which was a simply amazing leap forward in handling for the time. Without a dyno, if you simply make changes to a damper piston and get lucky, you won't know what the change in force it was that had the impact you wanted, therefore making subsequent changes more difficult.

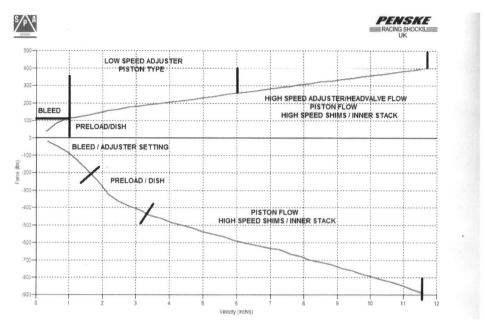

Penske force deflection curve showing which parts of the curve are affected by which component.

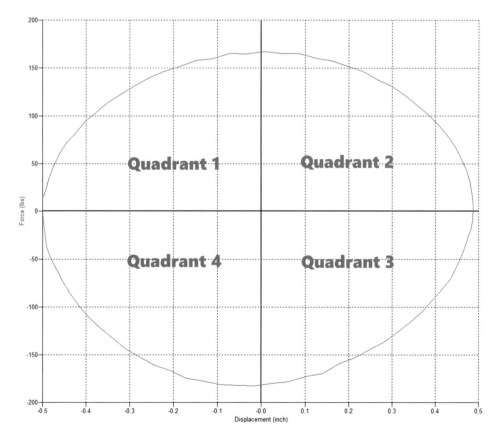

SPA dyno output showing the four damper quadrants.

DYNO GRAPH OVERVIEW – COURTESY PENSKE SHOCKS

Quadrant 1

This is the beginning of the compression stroke: it begins where the graph crosses the zero line (pounds) in quadrant #1. Typically the first ½in (12.7mm) of displacement is formed with relation to the low-speed bleed bypass. When the shaft reaches a certain velocity, the low-speed bleed bypass chokes off and the compression valve stack begins to react.

Quadrant 2

This quadrant begins with the compression valve stack open. The point where the graph crosses the zero line (inches) in quadrant #2 is where maximum force is produced by the compression valving. As the shock approaches the full compression point, the compression valve stack begins to close as it approaches the rebound movement.

Quadrant 3

This quadrant begins with the shock at full compression and the compression valve stack closed. The rebound stroke begins where the graph crosses the zero line (pounds) in quadrant #3. Approximately the first [1/2]in (12.7mm) of displacement is formed with relation to the rebound bleed through the shaft and jet. When the shaft reaches a certain velocity, the bleed chokes off and the rebound valve stack begins to react.

Quadrant 4

This quadrant begins with the rebound valve stack open. The point where the graph crosses the zero line (inches) in quadrant #4 is where maximum force is produced by the rebound valving. As the shock approaches the full extension point, the rebound valve stack begins to close as it approaches the compression movement. At this point the cycle starts over again in quadrant 1.

AERODYNAMIC SPRINGS

In most formulae where aerodynamics are key to speed, a spring that is there to absorb aerodynamic downforce only is prohibited. In the 1960s Jim Hall, a distinguished engineer, pushed the automotive field forward with his pioneering and innovative racing-car designs. This culminated in 1966 with his revolutionary 2E model, which incorporates features that modern F1 cars use to this day.

What is most notable, though, is that the wing design was mounted in such a way that the springs did not take the aerodynamic load. Of course this naturally provides better performance, as it doesn't require excessively stiff springs to absorb aerodynamic load. By pressing a floor-mounted pedal, it was possible to reduce the angle of attack on the wing as well as change the flow of air through the nose to reduce drag (and downforce).

A damper engineer must then consider not just the loads from all the freedoms of movement on the vehicle, but also the aerodynamic loads placed on the vehicle. It is very likely that once you start adding downforce, you'll run out of travel on the suspension. To some degree this can be helped with stiffer springs, but eventually the natural frequencies can be too much for the tyre, and it is better to use a bump stop that increases the rate but will only be engaged during very high g-cornering or during long straights with significant downforce.

BUMP STOPS

At very high forces the damper will reach the limit of its travel. Most assemblies will employ some kind of bump stop, which will generally be made from a closed cell polyurethane (PU)-type foam.

Traditionally, before the advent of PU foam bump stops, rubber was used. This tended to result in a rapidly rising rate, which could make the vehicle difficult to control in a limit-handling situation. The benefit of PU foam is that it can be made in a myriad of different shapes and sizes to offer a truly progressive rate in force versus deflection. Although the majority of roll control is gained from the anti-roll

A Chapparal 2e on display at Petroleum Basin Museum.

Polyurethane foam bump stop on a Penske damper.

VELOCITY M/S	REBOUND FORCE (N)	COMPRESSION FORCE (N)
0.05	380	240
0.26	1065	860
0.52	1350	1130

Bilstein damper force versus velocity for VW Golf road car.

bar, using too stiff a bar can cause both traction and comfort issues over single wheel bumps (both less of a concern on a smooth circuit). Bump stops are very useful aids to controlling the on-limit behaviour of the car. When the spring rate is overcome and the bump stop makes contact, the wheel rate will rise.

Engineers will tend to design a road car with relatively low wheel frequencies, lots of preload to hold up the car, and then a progressive PU bump stop that is integral to the vehicle's suspension performance. The PU bump stop enables a modern passenger car to combine a comfortable ride with excellent on-limit wheel control. The progressive rate of the PU bump stop can ensure that roll angles are limited, which pays dividends, particularly with MacPherson strut suspension where camber control through compression is a weakness.

Your first thoughts may be that the damping rates won't be enough to control the much higher rate of the bump stop, and it's not until you see damping rates versus velocity that you start to realize how high the forces are with higher velocities. For example, look at this analysis of a Bilstein damper for a Mk6 VW Golf GTI (pictured above). At 0.05m/s (2in per second), the force the damper generates is 240N (54lb) on compression and 380N (85lb) on rebound. Up the velocity to a high-speed event at 0.52m/s, and you see a rebound force of 1,350N (303lb) and a compression force of 1,130N

(254lb), both significantly higher than the standard spring rate on such a vehicle.

It's a sobering thought that in extremis, rally cars jumping into the air and landing can produce velocities exceeding 3m/s. It's extremely hard to control that kind of velocity, and to some extent the driver is in the lap of the gods.

ANTI-ROLL BARS

Anti-roll bars are fitted to the vast majority of production saloons and specialist sports cars. There is no easier way to provide such a wide range of roll stiffness adjustment, and consequently weight transfer. If you go searching online you'll often find discussions about designing chassis where no anti-roll bar is required. Unless the vehicle has some other form of roll control – for example, McLaren dispense with anti-roll bars through their use of a hydraulic suspension system that is interconnected between wheels, providing re-active roll control – then the chances are that with no anti-roll bars it would behave worse.

Changing the stiffness of the anti-roll bar can be achieved with a number of methods. The simplest is a blade with multiple holes drilled in, and on the after-market you will find a number of manufacturers such as H&R and Whiteline making anti-roll bars that are both larger and adjustable.

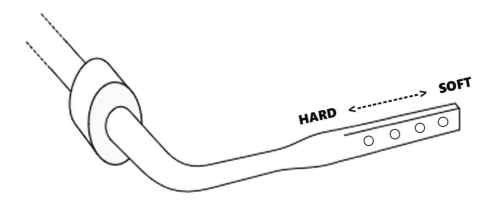

HARD <----------> SOFT

Adjustable anti-roll bar.

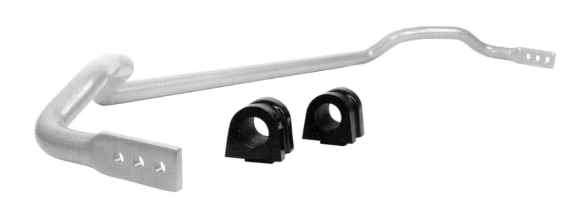

An uprated front anti-roll bar with force adjustment via multiple droplink connection positions.

The aim will be generally to reduce outright roll, but also potentially to increase maximum cornering force by better optimizing the tyre contact patch, and the weight transfer around the chassis. For example, on a front-wheel-drive vehicle the manufacturer will have incorporated an amount of understeer into the chassis which they feel is safe not only for all drivers, but also takes into consideration under-inflated tyres, overloading, and violent steering inputs. The lap timer really is the best way to understand how changing roll stiffness can make the car faster. Typically to gain more outright cornering speed on a front-wheel-drive car, more rear roll stiffness will be needed.

On a rear-wheel-drive car the chances are that both front and rear roll stiffness should be increased, but often more percentage increase on the rear is needed. This helps balance out the more benign nature of many rear-wheel-drive front ends. As the accelerator can be deployed, changing the handling balance, most rear-wheel-drive cars tend to be set up with the front end slightly softer than a really sporting front-wheel-drive hot hatch, for example, which will tend to want to change direction much more readily via the steering wheel.

If you purchase an after-market bar you will hopefully be buying into a product that has been thoroughly tested, and found to improve the vehicle in the way you desire. However, often this isn't the case, as TUV test regulations, to which much of Europe adheres, can get in the way of optimal development. For example, they take the lowest common denominator behind the wheel as the test basis – that is, a complete novice with no car control or finesse on the limit whatsoever. This can mean that there is still too much understeer in a chassis for racetrack performance. So just because a product seems to be marketed as fit for racing, this doesn't necessarily mean it is optimized for that environment.

The best solution is testing. Using a tyre temperature gauge and lap times as well as 'seat-of-the-pants' feel and feedback from the driver, will enable you to get the right size bars adjusted correctly.

THE FUTURE

It is sad that Citroën have abandoned their hydropneumatic suspension system, but it doesn't mean the dream of active suspension isn't alive. The Tenneco system fitted to the McLaren P1 is arguably a fully active system, and the chances are that this type of set-up will become more popular on premium products. They may have stopped using it at the time of press, but Citroën still license their system to other manufacturers, so it has not really gone.

Simpler systems, such as Maserati's Skyhook Suspension system, which is adaptive damping and can provide anti-dive, anti-squat and anti-roll, are likely to filter down into more models. However, until the regulations in motor sport change, it seems that a lot of the technology won't be available on circuit cars. Perhaps the drive towards electric propulsion (particularly with torque vectoring) and autonomous vehicles will further the adoption of more sophisticated suspension systems.

For example, the latest Lamborghini Huracan employs the Lamborghini Dinamica Veicolo Integrata (LDVI) system, a CPU that controls the car's dynamics via various systems to try and anticipate the needs of the driver. A kind of 'chassis AI', if you like, the promise being 'perfect driving dynamics'. Not dissimilar to the sensors on a Hydractive 3 Citroën system, the more seductively named Lamborghini Piattaforma Inerziale (LPI) deploys a comprehensive set of accelerators and gyroscope sensors at the centre of gravity. LPI monitors in real time the vehicle's dynamic attitude with regard to lateral, longitudinal and vertical accelerations, as well as roll, pitch and yaw rate.

A feed-forward processing logic is deployed by the LDVI, which actually means the car is trying to predict the handling set-up the driver wants. As well as changing the handling via the damping, it can also change the drive train via torque vectoring, thus controlling yaw, and can in addition change the steering response. This would seem to solve one of the areas of compromise for the vehicle dynamics engineers, in that they must develop their product to the lowest common denominator (that is, to be safe in the hands of a terrible driver). If a suspension system is adaptive to the driver, then an inexperienced driver whose inputs are too large and clumsy can be catered for by adaptively changing the set-up to bring the car under a safer set of handling parameters.

There is, of course, often the argument amongst professional drivers and reviewers that simple cars without complicated control systems are more thrilling to drive. Just recently Chris Harris of *Top Gear* fame announced that the most special car he owned was a simple Peugeot 205 Rallye with just a front-wheel-drive chassis, no driver aids, and on paper, a flawed chassis with its pure trailing-arm rear suspension.

What this means, though, is that, for a keen driver, on the open road it has a very low level of steady-state understeer, mainly due to the rear suspension design. This makes the car feel very direct, with a love of direction changes. However, they can catch out the unwary, due to the predilection for lift-off oversteer.

Chris Harris says his most special car is this Peugeot 205 Rallye.

Hyundai elevate concept car. HYUNDAI MOTOR COMPANY

One of the areas that a lot of modern cars are developing is the choice of driver modes. Sometimes these are gimmicky, but with the increasing penetration of more sophisticated adaptive and even active systems it could well be the case that a true driver's car could be locked just a few modes away from the standard system suitable for all. The ride quality in a modern McLaren super car over a rough road is nothing short of amazing, particularly given its high G capability on smooth tarmac. But with a price tag as much as a house you could live in, we are still some way away from this technology being mainstream. You could argue that Citroën did all this years ago, and nobody noticed. However, having a good idea doesn't mean it will be popular, and conversely, a bad idea can be very lucrative. Witness the popularity of the SUV, which in nearly all areas is beaten comprehensively by the equivalent saloon, yet consistently outsells it.

It is likely that once active suspension starts to permeate its way through more brands, it will become the norm. Then perhaps the motor-sport governors, seeing it so commonplace, will permit its use at all levels. This is difficult to say for sure, though, as witness how ABS on a motorcycle is a wonderful invention, yet most motorbikes shun its benefits.

The answer probably depends on how radical future transport is. Consider the Elevate concept from Hyundai – its four wheels can be moved through five freedoms of motion, enabling it to crawl literally up a mountain. Not only could this have a dramatic impact for rescue missions into hostile terrain, but it could also see a family hatchback transform into a genuine off-road vehicle.

If this became the norm on the road, then surely active suspension is going to be allowed again in Formula 1?

SET UP, TEST, RINSE AND REPEAT

Buying suspension components and installing them is relatively easy, particularly if the vehicle is well catered for. But unfortunately it is only part of the puzzle. Take, for example, the installation of a set of

'coil-over' dampers. These facilitate adjustment of spring preload to change the ride height.

Many manufacturers will supply a useful manual showing the user where to set the spring seat. More often than not, though, people will then use the tape measure between the centre of the wheel and the arch. They will then try to ensure the car is level on all four corners. If the car has anti-roll bars fitted, these will now start to move load around the car. So you'll see that increasing the right rear (RR) by 5mm may well then move the left rear (LR) up by a similar amount.

What usually ends up happening is that a range of adjustment up and down will be made, and then the car will often be wedged to one diagonal.

Wedge is the term used to describe a bias in cross-weight, where the right front (RF) and LR tyres carry more load than the left front (LF) and RR. Now if you are in the USA you tend to run anti-clockwise, so the car will be wedged in for LF and RR high. Other countries also run counter clockwise, mostly due to driving on the right-hand side of the road and having the steering wheel on the left-hand side. This is perhaps a good way of visualizing how the wedge can work. A right-hand-drive car you will have noticed turns best around right-hand turns, and of course the opposite is true of a left-hand-drive car.

Wedge is only useful if you are turning in one direction for all the corners. Perhaps on a circuit with just one left-hand corner it could be argued it is worth biasing for right only, however it depends how critical that left-hand corner is – if it's a slow corner followed by a long straight it is a crucial corner to be quick on.

So for turning left and right, the usual practice is 50 per cent cross weight on the scales. The best way to do the primary set-up before scaling is to adjust the spring seats so they are in the same position for each axle pair – that is, the FR matches the FL and the RL matches the RR. If you do this when the car goes on the scales, the cross weight will be close to 50 per cent. Typically you'll find that an adjustment to the tune of 1–2 per cent is required when the car is set up this way. If set by the ride height, then 5

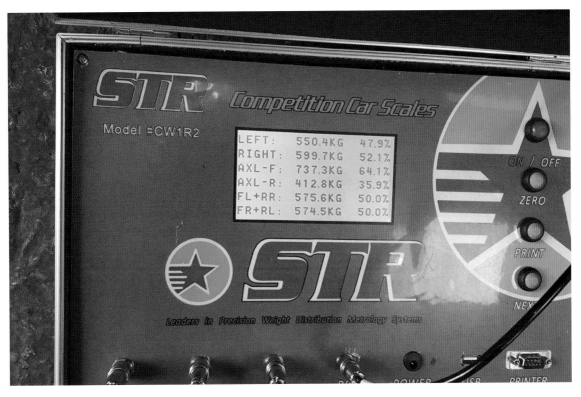

Picture of corner-weight scales with car set to 50 per cent cross weight.

per cent + adjustment is required – which is a lot of weight in the wrong place.

Geometry is a crucial part of set-up strategy, where the objective is to have the fastest time. Using the tyre temperatures as your guide, select a camber angle to optimise the grip from the tyre. Toe change should be used cautiously, particularly on the rear axle, where a small amount of toe-in is healthy to avoid instability under braking, when the wheels will tend to toe out. On the front axle having a small amount of toe-out can help, except perhaps when the circuit tends to have long straights and is naturally high speed.

You need to devise a system for recording data, and use this to analyse and improve your performance. This is probably the most important part of your suspension adventure: no matter what formula you are competing in, or how much you've spent, accurate and consistent measurement of changes is the secret to revealing the best performance from you and the vehicle.

When testing was reduced in Formula One, you can imagine the need for accurate modelling and simulation off the track. Most competitors in less hallowed formula will be relying on data gathered on the track.

It was tempting to follow the path of a flow chart for this section. However, there are cases where trusting implicitly the choices that a flow chart gives you, can lead you to a dead end. For example, with regard to damping, if you had understeer on corner entry you might be able to solve this by adding low-speed compression damping to stabilize the axle and get more initial weight transfer. Conversely, you may find you already have enough low-speed compression damping, and that any more contributes to more understeer.

The real problem with any kind of flow chart is that it doesn't take account of the foibles and virtues of the different suspension systems. They also don't have an agreed starting point. For example, there is no universally accepted percentage of critical damping starting point. How an adjustment up or down on an individual damper will affect the vehicle is dependent on the granularity of the adjustment and its position before adjustment. You will find that sealed tarmac courses permit much higher damper settings than more undulating and uneven surfaces, where higher settings usually lose grip.

It is helpful to discuss set-up anomalies. Ordinarily stiffening a rear anti-roll bar will create more weight transfer about that axle. Assuming the front end of the vehicle is generating as much grip as it can, then stiffening the rear axle is likely to make the rear of the car more mobile. However, a side effect of reducing roll is that extension and compression of the suspension are also reduced. If the vehicle had a suspension system that suffered from excessive toe change on compression and extension, then adding the stiffer rear anti-roll bar may actually increase rear grip. Increasing rear grip is a way to stop understeer. So this is a good example of how a flow chart that says 'rear axle – increase rear anti-roll bar stiffness – increase oversteer' is too simplistic.

You will recognize that you are on the right lines when you can look through handling flow charts and question the wisdom they offer, by changing the assumptions that were made. For example, talking about 'static negative camber setting' takes on new importance if you are dealing with an archaic trailing-arm style suspension, where the roll angle will equal the camber angle. In this instance the anti-roll bar doesn't just play its part in balancing the handling attitude of the chassis, it also becomes a key dynamic geometry enhancement aid.

DAMPER SET-UP

When thinking about damper set-up it is helpful to remember that compression and rebound will have different effects, at different points of the corner. If a series specifies a control damper that isn't adjustable, one of the biggest benefits is that you can just focus on every other area of set-up. Sprints and hillclimbs are very free in terms of suspension modification, so you could have three-way or even four-way,

rather than try and provide a prescriptive chart to help you solve your handling ailment, particularly as most of them don't tell you the suspension or drive layout of the car, nor provide its handling compliances. It is best to discuss it, so you can visualize dynamically what is happening.

CORNER ENTRY

On the way into a corner as the car is transitioning from braking to turning, it is compression damping on the front, and rebound damping on the rear that controls the weight transfer into the corner. If the car is tending to suffer from corner entry understeer and you have control over rebound and compression damping independently, then it is best to change compression on the front and rebound on the rear. If you have a two-way damper the chances are that compression adjustment will operate in the low piston speed range. The high-speed adjustment enables you to get the best response over kerbs and bumps.

MID-CORNER

As the car enters the turn and lock is applied, due to the caster in the chassis the RF wheel pushes down into the tarmac, aiding grip, while on the LR the load is also increased. If the car is only going in one direction, then it is possible to offset the damper set-up, much like the corner weights – in which case ensuring there isn't too much RF rebound or LR compression may help on a clockwise oval. If the car is suffering from understeer or oversteer in the mid-corner range but had no issues on corner entry, this is probably best solved by other chassis changes, as it probably points to a share of weight transfer issue more than a damper setting (for example, mid-corner oversteer may point to too much rear roll stiffness, or too little front).

The reason for this is the dampers have most impact in transitional phases of cornering. You can reduce roll on the way into a corner, but once the car loads up round the middle of the corner, the outside will be close to maximum compression, and the inside dampers at maximum extension. This is why minimizing droop can control roll, and also prevent a loss of traction on the inside wheel. Excessive droop levels will see too much body roll, and wheelspin on the lightly loaded inside wheel.

CORNER EXIT

The exit is a crucial phase of the corner, and one the damper can help tremendously with. As a mirror image of corner entry, with acceleration being the driving factor, the settings that work depend on which axle is driven. As a rear-wheel drive exits a corner, it will gain traction by having less front rebound damping and less rear compression damping, from a setting that was too high. Note the last quote – from a setting that was too high: imagine if the front rebound was too high, but the rear compression was too low in a front-wheel drive – this would be a calamity, and yet in a rear-wheel drive this might not matter too much, because at least weight can move to the rear easily and aid traction.

Imagine we are exiting one corner and then about to take another in quick succession. We want the vehicle to stabilize quickly, but the dampers on the outside of the turn will be in a rebound phase, and the dampers on the inside turn will be in a compression phase. Compared to road use, the dampers may be turned up significantly more, to cope successfully with the greater stored energy in extension from the outside wheels.

However, too much rebound damping is going to affect that transition and prevent the bodyshell from unloading to the other side. The weight will still transfer, but the damper could slow the transfer too much, and you end up with the car doing something unruly, as it seems out of sync with your inputs. Perhaps liken it to the swing-axle response in extremis, or a canal barge that still seems to be going one way, when you are trying to go another.

On the flip side, if you have too little rebound damping and compression damping you might find the weight transfer a little too quick. Think about how a production car with modest aspirations behaves on track. Usually the damper does little to slow roll, as the settings have been chosen to promote comfort.

If there was an agreed standard of baseline damper setting, in order to make flow charts more useful, perhaps the starting point might be a typical family car that isn't already set up for more sporting purposes. This is perhaps more meaningful than proposing damping set to 30 per set of critical level as a start point, as this means the discussion is biased to engineers, and most of us are not engineers. The vast majority of cars are designed to be used by drivers of all skills and abilities on a variety of surfaces. They need good suspension travel, and damping that is soft enough to permit comfort over this wide range of conditions.

So on circuit it would be fair to say that adding more compression and rebound damping from this baseline would add grip. Go too far, though, and the grip slides away and transitional handling becomes less predictable.

UNDERSTANDING KART SET-UP CAN IMPROVE CAR SET-UP

If you read texts online about reducing understeer or oversteer, you'll quickly get a feel for which changes will make a difference. You may even have remembered most of them, so that when you are at a circuit and you are suffering from understeer in a car, you may well stiffen the rear roll bar, and soften the front.

However, there are occasions when set-up changes do not have the desired effect, and quite often it can help to go back to basics and consider the way the kart works. For example, a car could be suffering from understeer. Various modifications have been made to reduce understeer (increasing rear roll stiffness, widening the front track, softening the front springs), and yet the driver is still complaining of understeer. Perhaps they might even say the tyre temperatures are all right. In many cases tyre temperatures won't be checked, but when they are, they may well show that the front tyres are not getting enough heat to work properly. So the car world thinks 'widen track – increase corner speed'.

However, in the kart world it's all about the tyres, and if they aren't 'in the zone', then just as in F1, things aren't working. All the changes that in a car were supposed to add front-end grip may well cost it in a kart, if the tyre doesn't get hot enough or have the right contact point. It's not that they are completely different, it's just that with suspension and a differential a car behaves very differently to a kart. Possibly in this instance all the changes that have been made, that should have dialled out the understeer, are actually making it worse, because the tyres are simply not getting up to working temperature.

This is why in the sphere of kart set-up, front track is usually narrowed to dial out understeer to generate more front weight transfer, increase the heat of the tyre, and increase grip. Not having any suspension system, the tyre in a kart is the effective suspension, acting as an undamped spring. The way the tyre works is so critical to a kart that arguably some karters are better at chassis set-up than many club motor-sport racers.

TO SUM UP...

The best way to set up a chassis is to use all the knowledge available in order to start with a good baseline, then make one change at a time, and record the improvement (or lack of it) – just like a scientific experiment. It is then a case of 'rinsing and repeating' until you make headway. Any hiccups along the way are valuable learning opportunities. Try not to get too wrapped up in prescriptive flow charts, as they can lead you to a dead end, where your conversation runs along the lines of 'we've tried everything to get rid of understeer, and yet we still have understeer'.

The question you most want to ask, in the face of that statement, is whether they were at the front or the back of the grid. The majority of professional drivers prefer a little understeer to lean on. This is particularly true of any high-speed car, where both suspension geometry and aerodynamics come into play. If you consider the fine art that Porsche has made of endurance racing over more than fifty years, it is useful to consider just how bad the original 917 was: it was literally lethal.

If you are feeling out of your depth in a competitive environment, it is always worth remembering that in most sports, perseverance counts for much more than natural talent. You can create a racer just as you can create a fighter. If a driver is a hothead, surround them with calming influences to ensure this tendency doesn't get the better of them. If your first race car is desperately slow and spins off into the gravel trap, don't give up.

Correctly setting up a car to work at a given circuit is a bit like setting a graphic equalizer on the sound system to match, and work with, the acoustics of the room. When you speak to people in the racing industry, it is clear that even at the highest levels there are significant differences between driver styles and preferences. They can be poles apart in the set-up and specification, and yet within fractions of a second on the track. This is arguably what makes this such a fulfilling area of a vehicle, as there is real art and science at work at the same time.

Try making some changes, and see what results you get. Milliken brought the science of aeronautical engineering to the automotive world. Perhaps your discipline has something about it that can help advance our learning in this area. Whatever your line of work now, sheer hard work rarely fails to get you ahead.

INDEX

Ackermann angle 130
active suspension 44–5
adaptive suspension 46–7
adjustable dampers 30–36
aerodynamic springs 164
aligning torque 134
anti-dive and anti-lift geometry
    124
anti-roll bars 34–5, 166–8

beam axle 90
Bilstein mono-tube dampers
    50–59
Bilstein unit 82
BMC hydragas system 42
BMC hydrolastic system 42
brief history of suspension, a
    8–10
bump steer 132–3
bump stops 164–6
Bundorf analysis 134
Bundorf, R.T. 134

camber 116–21, 131–2
camber versus lateral load 140
car set-up 173–4
caster 121–3
chassis engineers 162
chassis stiffness 104–7
circle of grip 17–18
Citroën system 37–41
coil-over kit 61
contact patch 18–19
control arms 61

damper set-up 172–3
    corner exit 173
    corner entry 172
    mid-corner 172–3

damper specification sheet 144
dampers 25–36
    upgrading 141–3
damping 25–36
    curve, modifying and adjusting
        145–7
    curve, setting the 143–4
    forces 25–8
    the function of 10
    the importance of 141–3
Dean, James 95
De Dion 88–90
DIY damper tuning 150–58
double adjustable damper 32
double wishbone suspension
    88–9
drifting 18
dynamic negative camber 126
dyno graphs, interpreting 162–4
dyno testing 158–61

EDFC Active Pro 47–9

Fiat Panda 100HP test car 61–85
flutter shim stack 148
four-way adjustable damper 36
future of car suspension 168–70
Fy compliance steer 134

G-Force 10, 18, 121
Gaz Shocks 147, 150
geometry 171
grip 16–22
    complexitites of 16–17
    managing the circle of 21
    the circle of 17–18

hydractive system 40–41
hydraulic dampers 28–30

hydro-pneumatic suspension
    36–40
hydro-pneumatic systems, the
    future 43–4
hysteresis 23–5

included angle 131–2
independent trailing arm 94
introduction 6–7

jacking forces 95

kart set-up 173–4
kinematic summary 141
Krebs, Arthur 121

Leffert, R. L. 134
live axle 88–90
load transfer effect 134
Lotus 44–5

MacPherson strut 87–8
Magès' system 36–7
McLaren 42–3
mechanical aero suspension 49
Mercedes-Benz 119–20
Milliken, William F. 117–18
monotube damper 29–30

negative camber 120–21
negative scrub 129
notched shims 149

overturning moment, the 21–2

Panhard rod 91
Penske damper, rebuilding a
    150–58

Penske Racing UK (Spa Design) 143–4, 145, 146, 147, 149, 150–58, 160–61, 164
pitch optimization 107–15
pneumatic trail 18–21
pull-rod suspension 96–7
push-rod suspension 96–7

rate-plate shim stack 148
roll camber 134
roll centre height 133
roll steer 132–3, 134
rubber suspension 23–4
Ruggieri, Alex 143–4, 145

SAT compliance steer 134
scrub radius 126–9
set-up strategy 171
shim-stack tricks 148–9
shim-stack worksheet 55–9
shock absorbers 25–36
shot peening 22–3
single adjustable damper 30–31
sliding axle 96
sliding pillar 96
Society of Engineers (SAE) 133
Spa Design 143–4, 145, 146, 147, 149, 150–58, 160–61
spring rates 97–101

springs 22–3
    materials 22
    protective treatment 23
    winding a 22
Steering Axis Inclination (SAI) 126–9, 131–2
surfaces 10
    bumpy 13–15
suspension
    arms 60
    bushes 61
    frequency 101–4
    geometry: camber 116–21
    layouts 86–101
    springs 60
swing axle 94, 96

TEIN 47–9
    EDFC system 47–9
Tenneco kinetic system 42–3
three-way adjustable damper 32–3
toe angle 132
toe versus lateral load 140
toe versus MZ 140–41
torsion beam axle 90, 94
trail 121–3
twin-tube damper 28–9

tyre and wheel axis systems 135–6
    earth-fixed coordinate system 135
    intermediate axis system 135
    reference frame 135
    road axis system 136
    road plane 136
    vehicle access system 136
    vehicle plane of symmetry 136
    vehicle reference frame 136
tyres 16–22
    grip versus vertical load 20
    temperatures 120
    testing 21

upgrading dampers 141–3

vehicle dynamics 136–41
    modelling 133–6

walking frequency 103
Watts linkage, the 92–3
weight jacking 125–6
wheel rate 98–101
Williams 45–6

yaw 136–40